STREETCARS

O F

FLORIDA'S FIRST COAST

STREETCARS

OF

FLORIDA'S FIRST COAST

ROBERT W. MANN

Foreword by Glorious J. Johnson

THE
History
PRESS

Published by The History Press
Charleston, SC 29403
www.historypress.net

First published 2014

Manufactured in the United States

ISBN 978.1.62619.707.7

Library of Congress Cataloging-in-Publication Data

Mann, Robert W.
Streetcars of Florida's First Coast / Robert W. Mann.
pages cm
Includes bibliographical references and index.
ISBN 978-1-62619-707-7 (paperback)
1. Electric railroads--Cars--Florida--Jacksonville Region--History. 2. Street-railroads--
Florida--Jacksonville Region--History. 3. Jacksonville Region (Fla.)--History. 4. Atlantic
Coast (Fla.)--History, Local. I. Title.
TF725.J33M36 2014
388.4'6097591--dc23
2014036895

For my wife, Libia, with love. I am keenly aware of your innermost feelings. However, it was according to the dictates of time and publication deadlines that I resolved to finish this book for all the generations to come. By enduring the unendurable and suffering what was unsufferable, through all of the lonely days and nights, you have been a bright beacon of inspiration.

...As a salute to one of our favorite adopted sons, Oliver "Babe" Hardy, who got his start in show business in Jacksonville, the chapter titles in this book are taken from his many movies and shorts.

Above, left: Jacksonville Traction pass. *Courtesy of the Professor Seth Bramson Collection.*

Above, right: Weekly passes were introduced at the opening of the South Jacksonville Muni. Pass number one was issued to the mayor of Jacksonville and number two to the mayor of South Jacksonville. *Courtesy of the Professor Seth Bramson Collection.*

Left, top: The later Jacksonville City Coach Company badge is a bit more brazen as City Coach Lines was a National City Lines subsidiary. Making use of an image of the statue of "youth" from Jacksonville's Memorial Park was perhaps a subtle boast that it had indeed conquered their world. *From the author's collection.*

Left, bottom: Motor Transit Company badge stressing the "wonderful service" to be had after the rubber tire victory. *From the author's collection.*

"To the United States belongs the honor of the paternity of the street railway, which now forms so important a factor in the life of all the cities of the modern world."
—Railway Age *Magazine*

"I see in electric motors possibilities for the future of the street car [sic] business of the country that must revolutionize the entire system of conducting it by means of horses."
—C.A. Richards

"I don't know when I will find time to get down that way, although I often think of and wish that I could be there again. Even though I am in California, my heart is in Florida; the best times of my life were spent in Jacksonville."
—Oliver N. "Babe" Hardy

CONTENTS

CONTENTS

FOREWORD

Robert "Bob" Mann is one of the most impressive people I know when it comes to streetcars, trains and mass transportation. I have had the honor and pleasure to know this fantastic man who cares so much about making transportation better for the people to go to work, play, worship and travel. Bob gives an excellent historical perspective in *Streetcars of Florida's First Coast* that includes many of the challenges faced by the early developers of the region and serves as a chronicler of historical events.

The story is much more than a tale of rail vehicles and nostalgia; it gives us a historical record of the development of our neighborhoods, cities and region. The reader will find many familiar, even famous, names ranging from Henry M. Flagler and St. Elmo Acosta to General Motors president and CEO, Alfred P. Sloan and Roger Rabbit. In this book that is packed with intrigue, the reader will discover that one of the greatest systems of mobility ever devised did not die a natural death—it was murdered. Unscrupulous corporate dealings and heavy-handed micromanagement at the municipal level, hints of outright political corruption, FBI transcripts, indictments and convictions finish the tale.

An award-winning author, Robert's affectionate treatment of the streetcar systems is not one of a living organism; rather, it is as the arteries of mobility on which the living city is built. Robert builds a strong case for the success of streetcars as a development or redevelopment tool and explains why the same results cannot be had with modern buses.

Drawing on his broad experience in virtually every form of transportation and a personal library that could fill a streetcar barn, he leaves us with some

When Jacksonville Transit Authority emptied the old streetcar barn and hauled all of the files and artifacts to the city dump, it missed this coin changer given to the author by a former Jacksonville Traction Company conductor. *From the author's collection.*

important questions and offers some expert advice on how to recover what we have lost.

Robert is the father of contemporary efforts to rebuild street railways in Jacksonville and Northeast Florida, a fact that will surprise no one who reads his book. His presentation goes beyond a simple history lesson, and what he leaves us with may well be a manual to guide our urban future.

—Glorious J. Johnson
Jacksonville City Councilwoman, 2003–2011

PREFACE

I have had the honor to meet many of the great men of the old Jacksonville and other area traction companies. Studying history at various colleges and universities, including Jones College locally and Oklahoma State University, I've made many important friendships that have pushed this work along. Perhaps transportation is in my blood—I've worked for Piedmont and Continental Airlines, owned an Amtrak Express cartage company and served as a supervisor for Tamiami Trailways Bus System and the United States Postal Service. Finally, I began to work on transportation projects; a trip to my wife's native Republic of Colombia and her excellent connections put me face to face and later shoulder to shoulder with the inspector general of the national railroads.

In 1980, I was given the opportunity to address the Jacksonville Downtown Development Authority and present a plan for a reconstruction of a two-and-a-half-mile vintage streetcar. The DDA quickly adopted the concept as a project, and immediately we ran headlong into, as Lincoln said, "combinations too powerful to be suppressed by the ordinary course of judicial proceedings, or by the powers vested in the marshals by law." Reasoning that the downtown people mover was a free government gift and that the streetcars could derail that plan, the streetcar barn was leveled, and the five remaining streetcars around the city were reduced to sawdust. In the end, I was left jobless. A well-placed friend within the city visited at our home one evening in 1984 and said, "Bob, if you ever want to work again, get out of Jacksonville."

I no longer need them nor do I need employment. I do not seek revenge for any past wrongs, but for my beloved streetcars, I'm seeking a reckoning.

Having grown up in Ortega and Ortega Hills, this story excites my sensibilities of both what might have been and what could be. Be it the corruption and graft of 1932 or the treacherousness of the 1980s, this is a story that needs to be told.

ACKNOWLEDGEMENTS

This work would have been impossible without the amazing help and support of my wife and family. My colleagues and copublishers at metrojacksonville.com, true friends hidden within the Jacksonville Transportation Authority and City of Jacksonville as well as other city and county governments throughout the First Coast added infinite encouragement. To the Jacksonville Public Library downtown; Palatka Public Library; Carl S. Swisher Library at Jacksonville University; Thomas G. Carpenter Library at the University of North Florida; the Southern Historical Collection at the Louis Round Wilson Special Collections Library at the University of North Carolina, Department of Special Collections; Washington University Libraries and their amazing staffs—my apologies for wearing holes in your carpets. Thank you for the tolerance exhibited by the Library of Congress, Smithsonian Libraries and the Los Angeles and Minneapolis Public Libraries. Thank you to the Jacksonville City Council Records Division, Clay County Archives, Putnam County Courthouse, Jacksonville Historical Society, St. Augustine Historical Society, Putnam County Florida Historical Society, Clay County Historical Society, Light Rail Now, Indiana Historical Society, Pennsylvania Historical Society and Ohio Historical Society. The Cities of Palatka, Green Cove Springs, St. Augustine and Jacksonville all had contributions too numerous to recall. A smile and a wink at the Jacksonville Transportation Authority for the great debates, condescending shouting matches, lost public records and labeling the entire metrojacksonville team "a bunch of flying monkeys"—thanks for the humorous memories.

The American Public Transportation Association, Electric Railway Clubs of Florida, Electric Railroaders' Association, Central Electric Railfans' Association, Seashore Trolley Museum, Shore Line Trolley Museum, Branford Electric Railway Association, Denver Tramway Heritage Society, Platte Valley Trolley, Gomaco Trolley Company, Village of East Troy Electric Railway and Orange Empire Railroad Museum all offered unlimited clues, suggestions and material.

For a certainty, the fog of senility will cause me to omit some precious friend or acquaintance who gave of their time or themself in this effort, to wit: Ennis Davis; Dan Herbin; Stephen Dare; Arash Kamiar; Dr. Ignacio Restrepo; Dr. Filipe Calle; Patricio Degaudenzi; Dr. Doug Baker; Professor Seth Bramson; Assistant Professor Robert Cassanello; Emily Lisska; Meghan Powell; Councilwomen Glorious Johnson, Lori Boyer and Nancy Sikes-Kline; Alyssa Pierce; Liz Gurley; Don Hensley; James Boyle; John Regan; Joel McEachin; Ken Mitchroney; Roger Rabbit and his "invisible friend," E.P. Rentz; Jason Sharpe; Harvey Stone; Tim Timkin; Ron Chamblin; Mansuel White; Lauren Mosley; Vishitra R. Garig; Susan Sutton; Nicole Poletika; Mary E. Murphy; Larry Beaton; Thad Crowe; and many others.

INTRODUCTION

Though not exhaustive, this is a book I was compelled to write—indeed, encouraged to write—as it is a story that needs to be told. This is a story about a great urban electric railway and the city that was built on the back of its broad-gauge tracks.

More than transportation, the street railways were, and still are, literal city builders. Their near silent operation, massive capacity and infrastructure permanence attract billions of dollars in new development that would never appear along supposedly more flexible modes of transportation.

By 1900, Jacksonville, St. Augustine, Palatka, Fernandina Beach and Green Cove Springs all boasted some form of urban railway. St. Augustine and later Jacksonville would both have streetcar lines far into the country and operating on their own exclusive right of way, in the same manner as modern light-rail systems do today. In fact, along with the Manatee Light and Power Company, Coral Gables High Speed Line and Tampa's famed Jungle Trolley, these railways actually performed an interurban function. Florida's streetcar systems were small by any national comparison; Chattanooga, Tennessee, for example, boasted nearly three hundred miles of electric railways.

There were one hundred thousand streetcar vehicles and 45,000 miles of streetcar track in operation nationally by 1918. Wherever possible, the "streetcar" did not operate on the streets. Streetcars were successfully used as inducements by developers who built extensions into suburbia, itself a creation of the electric railway. Interurban railways peaked at 15,500 miles (some high speed) around 1915, where scarcely 2,100 miles existed in 1900.

MAIN LINE SCHEDULE

SUMMER SERVICE

Effective Jun

No. 30 Daily

ALL TRAINS AIR-CONDITIONED

Daylight Express

			PM
......Jacksonville............N.	Ar		6.1?
....South Jacksonville...........	Lv		6.03
.........Bowden................	Lv	f	5.5?
.........Sunbeam...............	Lv	f	5.4?
.........Greenland.............	Lv	f	5.4?
.........Bayard.....	Lv	f	5.4?
.........Durbin....	Lv	f	5.3?
.....St. Augustine	.v		5.1?
.....College Park.	.v	f	5.0?
...Tocoi Junction			

Before passes or tap cards, tokens were the coinage of the worlds transit systems. *From the author's collection.*

The growth was phenomenal, but as the country passed into its decadent decade in 1920, the national economy leveled off. In Florida, the twenties would roar on as the state experienced unprecedented growth for another six years.

As suddenly as it began, it ended. Cities had long seen the street railways as a resident milch cow to be used for mass transit, development, tax revenue and street paving on demand. Suddenly, all around the country, including throughout the First Coast, a conspiracy against the streetcars burst onto the stage. Huge sums of cash were deposited in local banks while the depositors strongly suggested that there should be no more credit for the street railways. Newspapers appeared on the streets aimed at discrediting the street railways and promoting buses. Politicians were handed checks while being photographed in front of burning streetcars, while in South Florida, they were all driving brand-new Cadillacs. Even to this day, there are paid "fellows" and "consultants" who make their living traveling from city to city with messages such as, "Rail is not a good fit in Jacksonville." They try and debunk what has become known as the "Great Streetcar Conspiracy," and it makes sense to the unwashed masses, flexible buses, modern automobiles and "free" highways called freeways. But if you drink from this pasquinian fountain, debunk if you will the indictments, the FBI transcripts, the arrests, arraignment, conviction and fines that cost America its urban mobility and our cities' futures.

Rail is as good a fit in Jacksonville today as it was in 1900; the same can be said for smaller communities such as St. Augustine, which suffers from mobility problems, or Palatka, which could use a city-building development tool and attraction.

Florida's streetcars are wrecked; nothing was spared as a greedy cabal swept across the land, promising a new level of prosperity, all the while taking us for a ride. This is that story.

TECHNICAL TALK

In every case, volts multiplied by the amperes will give the number of watts. A kilowatt is 1,000 watts. There are 746 watts in the familiar horsepower measurement, so that a kilowatt is, roughly, one and a half horsepower. Kilowatt-hours are the product of kilowatts multiplied by the number of hours during which the current is in use. Thus, a powerhouse with a dynamo delivering current to the line of one thousand amperes at 550 volts pressure is generating 550,000 watts, or 550 kilowatts. If these 550 kilowatts are furnished, on average, twenty hours daily, we get 11,000 kilowatt-hours for the daily output. The total for the year can be arrived at from the daily totals.

Two little boys clutch their tokens awaiting the streetcar on North Main Street, circa 1913. The company served the schools as well as served as an unofficial daycare service, which the retired streetcar men said led to many lasting friendships. *Courtesy of the Jacksonville Historical Society.*

In the early days of streetcar electrification, steam generation stations often powered a vast network of streetcar lines. In large systems such as in Jacksonville, two power plants were established. Both of Jacksonville's plants were located on Riverside Avenue on the property occupied today by the *Times-Union* publishing company.

Initially, these power plants typically generated power at six hundred volts DC (direct current); in fact, all of the distribution in the system at the time was at that potential. Attempts were made to correct greater line loss in the six-hundred-volt feeder system. This was critical because the farther from the power source, the less power was available from the trolley wire. Motors would slow or struggle to operate properly, lights dimmed and the car could slow to a crawl until it approached another feeder station whence it would speed up, only to slow again until the next feeder. They attempted to balance the economies of operating large generating stations over smaller ones to no avail. In the final analysis, it was discovered through careful testing that transmitting a consistent line power at six hundred volts was virtually impossible. At the same time, they discovered the power plant boilers that were needed to generate such an amount of power could actually be smaller or that the larger ones could operate far more efficiently if power was generated and transmitted in AC (alternating current). This, of course, led to the development of much more modern generating stations and efficient transmission of the power supply.

The new system would supply AC power to substations placed every-so-many miles apart at 1,200, 9,000 or 22,000 volts. The AC current was converted to 600 volts DC for railway operations. Some smaller community systems found it more economical to turn their entire power generation over to a municipal or private electric utility company. Systems as large as Jacksonville's, however, found far more benefit in having all of the generation and distribution for railway use in the hands of the railways employees.

PART I

JACKSONVILLE

1
YOU'RE DARN TOOTIN'

To find the root of the streetcar, one would have to turn back to biblical times. It is, in fact, very likely that the apostle Paul rode the "Diolkos."[1] The name Diolkos is translated from two Greek words, one meaning "across" and the other meaning "portage machine." This tramway was built in 600 BC and connected the Ionian Sea to the Aegean Sea across the Isthmus of Corinth, a distance of about five miles. Discovering as they did that a fixed guideway was more efficient, the ancient expression "as fast as a Corinthian" was coined.

Horses, mules or oxen were the predominant motive power throughout the world until the development of steam power. Steam, however, was an expensive innovation, and it quickly began to separate the single-purpose tram and urban railways from the heavy-haul multipurpose railroads. As the gap between rail cars and missions broadened—single cars versus many dozens of cars—the railroads and the early horsecar lines became more distinct from each other.

Essentially horse-drawn "city buses," omnibuses had already appeared in great number. The omnibus was virtually an international phenomenon born of necessity to move large crowds at the lowest possible cost and smallest spatial footprint

Horses, mules and oxen, pulling omnibuses and streetcars of that era, had a huge negative effect on urban life. Each of these large urban animals would leave ten pounds of manure and soak the streets with showers of urine daily. As a result of the antifriction properties of the

Car 142 of the Riverside and Pearl Line carries the new and all-important "pay as you enter" message as it traverses the loops on Jacksonville's Forsyth Street, aka the "Great White Way." *Courtesy of the Jacksonville Historical Society.*

waste byproduct, smooth street pavements were impossible, so sand, clay, brick and cobblestone were widely used. A simple slip and fall onto a stone or brick pavement, with a small break in the skin, could,

in the absence of antibiotics, spell one's demise. Wherever the animals went, they left deposits that attracted billions of the *Musca domestica*, or common houseflies. Implicated in the transmission of Linnaeus diarrhea, shigellosis, food poisoning, typhoid fever, dysentery, tuberculosis, anthrax, ophthalmia and parasitic worms, the search for a new means of motive power was as intense as the race to the moon

In the forefront of industrial development, forces behind the advancement of steam locomotion came up with a diminutive engine of a "0-4-4-wheel arrangement," known as "Forney's." But the Achilles' heel of the infernal machines was that they still smoked, hissed and chuffed, potentially terrorizing or even stampeding domestic animals. However, if a Lilliputian locomotive alone wasn't the answer, perhaps camouflage was, so they developed a streetcar-like vehicle body, covering a small Forney. But another drawback of these little engines was their weight on the rails

The second great innovation was that of the iconic cable car, the humble vehicle that has become a symbol of San Francisco today. While not yet perfection, as the vehicles were still unpowered, the transit industry was quickly arriving at what would become a logical solution. The cable car indeed offered an apparent solution to the basic problems of street railways. Unfortunately however, the cable car idea, as novel as it was, represented a prodigious capital investment and excessive maintenance budget, one that took the whole industry down a ten-year sidetrack.

According to a special report of the census bureau, by 1902, only 1.9 percent of the track miles operated in the United States were still gripping a cable.

Perhaps the revolution started with Leo Daft in Saratoga, New York, notable for his experimentation with electric power. In 1885, Daft brought about the first urban electric railway line in Baltimore, but his 120-volt DC system was woefully underpowered. Others experimented with high voltage systems, perilously using direct current and primitive wiring, a potentially lethal combination. Nevertheless, even considering these shortcomings, South Bend, Indiana; Montgomery, Alabama; and St. Joseph, Missouri, all shifted to these mysterious powers of electrodynamics.

Frank Julian Sprague was a genius; born in 1857, he attended the United States Naval academy in Annapolis, Maryland, and served as a naval officer. In 1883, Sprague left the navy to join forces as a technical assistant to Thomas Edison.

Sprague introduced the use of mathematical formulas as a replacement for trial-and-error experimentation, going on to develop practical electric motors and electrical current transmission devices. After a year of working with Edison and with many inventions to his credit, Sprague struck out on his own in the field of electric railway development. Perfecting a number of his ideas, he is credited with creating systems of automatic controls, improved energy systems, wheel suspensions, nonsparking motors and better brakes. His motors could maintain a constant rate of revolution with varying loads. Finally, as a coup d'état, Sprague strung wire overhead and then created a pulley to run on the wire at the end of what amounted to a modern-day extension cord.

The managers of the Richmond Union Passenger Railway in Virginia were believers and asked Sprague to install some twelve miles of his new system. It transcended even the most optimistic of expectations.

Perhaps the most memorable takeaway from Sprague's electric car experiments began as something of a local joke and introduced a new word to the English language. The good-natured citizens of Richmond watched as Frank's vehicles went back and forth trailing that long cord, and soon the comic witticisms started. "Say look fellows, Frank is trolling for passengers!" Trolling? Perhaps it was then that Sprague extended the "fishing pole" up to the wire and the word "trolling" became corrupted; no longer were these "trolling cars," they were, now and forever, trolleys.

The world's first successful, large-scale electric trolley installation opened for business on February 2, 1888, with huge celebrations. For the first time in history, America owned a transportation technology.

Within ten years, the horsecar would be mostly a memory; the flies, the smells, health hazards and frustratingly slow speeds vanished with it. Likewise, the cable car with its tremendous physical plant footprint and other sundry ramifications was, for all intents and purposes, history. By 1905, Frank Sprague's inventions would be clicking along on over twenty thousand miles of track. The electric streetcar was everywhere, and Florida's First Coast was no different.

2
THEIR PURPLE MOMENT

It seems almost incredible that there isn't a single transit station named for the man who started it all locally. This is no doubt a splendid opportunity for sidewalk art that has been thus far overlooked.

Mass transit in Jacksonville is fortunate to have its founding father's name carved into the pages of history. While the first pioneers no doubt had horses, mules and carts, the first true transit vehicle of any kind was said to have belonged to an enterprising "colored man named Sam Reed," along with his faithful companion, "a mule named John." Before the War of Northern Aggression, Sam provided all of the drayage services in the city. His wagon and noble mount was the UPS, FedEx, freighter, transportation authority, Checker Cab, passenger hauler and town hearse of his day.

Rowboats and small sailing boats came into their own about the same time as Sam and John's drayage and quickly grew in popularity as pleasure craft. According to local legend, they had reputations akin to the modern-day "submarine races," or the classic "our car died," excuse for young couples who seemed to frequently become marooned on distant landings along the local waterways.

Among the well-heeled citizenry, and again, just prior to that bloody conflict, the first sulkies and buggies began to appear. Of course, Florida was beef country and every bit as underpopulated, wild and dangerous as the old west. In fact, the infamous gunslingers John Wesley Hardin and John Henry "Doc" Holliday were Jacksonville regulars. Hardin actually owned

Bay Street in Jacksonville, with a Jacksonville Street Railway car passing construction crews laying crossing timbers along the tracks according to paving ordinances. *Courtesy of the Jacksonville Historical Society.*

a butcher shop (rather appropriately), and the Holliday family of nearby Valdosta used the Port of Jacksonville to move their crops. Strong and spirited saddle horses reigned supreme.

Rising from the ashes of war, Jacksonville was infused with Federal troops. Hemming Plaza, downtown's "micro Central Park" and onetime site of a Confederate Signal Corps tower, became a Yankee garrison. Many of the northern hoards crowding the streets wrote polished and glowing letters home. A subtropical "paradise found."

While the newfound population boom continued to heat up, the commercial omnibus, at first a welcome novelty, became a commonplace vexation.

The burgeoning population had long since outgrown Sam Reed's drayage, and most felt it was time for a decisive move up. And though the ubiquitous omnibus had long since taken its place in the city, the experience could leave one enervated.

"Then followed a scene that fully assured me that from 'the sublime to the ridiculous' is but a very short distance." So remarked one early traveler, who continued, "We had scarcely time to disembark [from the steamship] before our party was besieged…A number of drivers, who seize the opportunity of the presence of travelers, to get up a general mêlée, derogate vehicles, interchange choice epithets, and give each other a conventional cursing. One fellow, seizing me by the arm, said, 'Mr. McDonald, get into my coach with your party.'"[2]

The Jacksonville and Riverside Horse Railroad

The first effort to change the omnibus experience was right after the 1870 census; Jacksonville had achieved seven thousand persons and was feeling like a boomtown. A so-called paper company that was long on ideas and short on substantial investment tried to establish itself. The name of the Jacksonville and Riverside Horse Railroad actually suggested some solid thinking. Unfortunately, the project appears to have never come to fruition.

Jacksonville Horse Railroad

The Jacksonville Horse Railroad was chartered in December 1875. The company actually went well beyond the planning stage and began construction, but the effects of the Great Market Panic of 1873 were still being felt and finances for the project dried up, bringing it to a halt. Ultimately, the company allowed its franchise to lapse.

Jacksonville Street Railway

Henry Bradley Plant of the Plant System of Railroads, with his associates, incorporated the Jacksonville Street Railway Company. With Mr. Plant firmly at the reins, this time there was no doubt of success. Following this news, on January 11, the City of Jacksonville passed an ordinance granting the company a franchise and establishing the rules for operating in the city.

Streetcars in those early days resembled their later descendants, the form being perfected nearly from the start; they were, however, quite a bit smaller and much lighter. Generally they had but four wheels mounted atop a strong spring chassis, with platforms at one or both ends. The finish inside and

This photo was originally printed on a glass plate, backwards. We have corrected the scene for historical accuracy as the Jacksonville Street Railway car 27 and its operator pose near the Five Points picnic grounds at the end of the line. *Courtesy of the Jacksonville Historical Society.*

out was where they literally shined. Seats with reversible backs of cane or velvet were common, as were exotic woods. Some streetcars (often called Narragansett cars), were open air; others (known as bobtails) were fully enclosed. Some went so far as to have gold-leaf lettering. However primitive they may have seemed, their fitting and finish would make an absolute mockery of today's faux trolley buses, which in reality have more in common with the everyday potato chip truck.

In a travelers' guide to Florida written during that era, the city of Jacksonville was described thusly:

> *Jacksonville, is the commercial metropolis...It is a handsome and prosperous-looking city, covering a good deal of ground, and, particularly during the winter season, when all the hotels are thrown open to the thronging guests, it presents an animated and picturesque appearance that is quite exceptional in the South.*[3]

The city granted the Jacksonville Street Railway the rights to lay track on Bay, Catherine, Duval, Hogan, Forsyth and Julia Streets. Work began down

Bay Street from La Villa to Fairfield. A loop went up Hogan to Beaver to Clay and back to Bay. The patrons were thrilled to escape the dusty roadways and ride the "rapid transit" when the cars started rolling in the autumn of 1880. Pulled by mules, the streetcars were universally referred to as "hay burners" in the national vernacular of the day. Scheduled streetcars easily outclassed and beat out the previously mentioned omnibus experience. Primitive as mule cars may seem to us today, the city was bursting with pride over its street railway.

Within a short time, the Jacksonville Street Railway decided the compactness of its reach was counterproductive, so in a move to both elucidate and expand the system, track was removed from Catherine, Duval and Forsyth. A new line was extended toward East Jacksonville, the city of Fairfield and the fairgrounds. (At that time, the fairgrounds occupied a series of blocks bounded by Haines, Jessie, Talleyrand and Marshall Streets.) A further extension was laid on Hogan Street from Bay Street north to Beaver and then west to Clay.

By the end of 1886, the city had expanded so rapidly that the Jacksonville Street Railway extended its lines South over McCoy's creek to the end of May Street in present-day Five Points. The company erected carbarns in Brooklyn, just north of the end of Leila Street and directly west off of Commercial Street (today's Riverside Avenue and current site of the monorail maintenance facility).

Pine Street Railway

Just two years behind the Jacksonville Street Railway (JSRY) in 1882, Mr. B. Upton chartered the three-foot (narrow) gauge Pine Street Railway Company.

The Pine Street Line started at the corner of Bay and Pine Streets; the little cars climbed the hill straight north across Hogan's Creek and into Springfield, ending at Eighth Street, which at the time was considered way out in the forest. The line was complete and in operation within a year. In August 1884, the railway was leased to one G.A. Backenstoe, who immediately sawdusted Pine Street, followed by construction of a new restaurant and dining hall with provisions for dancing and a stating rink.

But the streetcar wouldn't survive on dance hall and restaurant traffic alone, and S.B. Hubbard and Associates, the developers of Springfield, absorbed the streetcar property as a development tool.

"Passing the Waterworks," so says a Main Street Railway four-wheel car as it reaches the end of the track. After the passenger boards, the motorman will step off, grab the rope and pull down the pole, walking it around to the rear of the car and then returning it to the wire. The crew will then flip the seat backs (called walk-over seats) to face in the other direction, and off they'll go. *Courtesy of the Jacksonville Historical Society.*

Ultimately, the new ownership extended the line eastward on Eighth Street to Walnut and then southward to First Street returning to Pine.

Change was immediately apparent: "The fact was, the road was well patronized, and its business is exclusively between the business portion of Jacksonville and the suburbs is the best evidence of the growth of the latter."[4] With the streetcar and developer working as one, Springfield took off like a flame doused in gasoline. To this day, rails' ability to foster growth makes it one of the pillars of development.

MAIN STREET RAILWAY

When the name of Pine Street changed to Main Street, the streetcar company changed its name too, becoming the Main Street Railway.

JACKSONVILLE AND LAVILLA STREET RAILWAY

During the first half of the 1880s, LaVilla was an independent city; it would give birth to the Jacksonville and LaVilla Street Railway in 1884.

This company laid tracks on Newnan Street from Bay to Forsyth and from Forsyth to Laura to Adams to Myrtle. Burch's Brickyard was located on the west end of the line, and the railway opened with a grand celebration on January 24, 1885.

The J&LVSRY had only operated about a year when Plant's Jacksonville Street Railway bought it out. Almost immediately, the Plant Company (JSRY) took up the track on Newnan, Forsyth, Laura and Adams east of Bridge Street (present-day Broad Street). It ran a line straight up Bridge Street from Bay to Adams to tie in the western suburbs with the rest of the system.

JACKSONVILLE AND SUBURBAN RAILWAY

This little road was chartered on July 1, 1882, to run from Bay Street at Ocean north to Duval, east to Washington and north on Washington to Union. Here it turned east on Union and ran past the old city cemetery to Campbell's Addition. The two bobtail mule cars and their teams went to work moving passengers as soon as the line was complete in 1885.

The Suburban Road operated the property on twenty-minute headways[5] (meaning a car every twenty minutes) and charged five cents for the privilege of riding. It only dispatched cars for two years before it was bought out by the Plant interests and became a branch of the JSRY in 1887.

Plant reconfigured the track layout somewhat, removing the tracks on Ocean and relaying them on Newnan Street.

G.W. Jones, business manager of the *Times-Union* newspaper had an idea loaded with promise. On February 6, 1887, Mr. Jones unleashed his idea in a newspaper article entitled "Let Us Dish California." The idea was to create a world exposition in Jacksonville. Throughout the next season, feverish letters and meetings were held with railroad and business principals throughout Jacksonville, the state of Florida, the Bahamas, the Caribbean, West Indies, Mexico and Central and South America. Members of the Jacksonville Board of Trade took the lead, and with the railroads writing checks, the Jacksonville Sub-Tropical Exposition came into being. It seemed as though the entire world was coming to our front door.

The amazing Sub-Tropical Exposition of the late 1880s was every bit the equal of today's World Fair expositions. *Courtesy of the Jacksonville Historical Society.*

There arose at the midway point of the Main Street Railway such a collection of exhibition buildings as rarely, if ever, seen in the world up to that time, filled with mystifying displays pulled from the four corners of the subtropical universe. Located in the Springfield Parks at the city waterworks, the main building alone covered nearly one acre of ground.

No expense was spared on architectural proportions, and six towers and an observatory reached by a winding stairway rose above it all. The views of Jacksonville from the observatory or towers were stunning. The center of the building featured a large octagon-shaped fountain. All five mammoth buildings and a Seminole Indian Camp were nestled in groves of lush tropical fruit and flora. A beautiful bridge carried the sidewalk over a man-made lake to the "County Building," erected by Pasco, Citrus and Hernando Counties.

Jacksonville would see the development of Florida's first theme park—the Jacksonville Alligator Farm. They called the native of India Joe, but his real name was Hubert Campbell. He was the son of an English officer.

Joe's star animal was known as Old Ocklawaha, and he spread the story that this beast was eight hundred years old and ate an astonishing one hundred pounds of fish a day.

In 1907, the animal menagerie marched out of the Phoenix Park neighborhood and landed on the Southbank at the huge Dixieland Park, operated by the ferry company and promoted by the street railways.

When Dixieland closed, victim of a disastrous freak hailstorm, Alligator Joe and his pets moved on to the site of today's Aetna and Baptist Medical Center complexes.

Joe Campbell died in 1926, only fifty-three years of age. Thirteen years later, his beloved farm was no more. In 1939, with the city rapidly surrounding the biggest tourist attraction in Florida, some six thousand alligators were crated and moved to Daytona Beach. Alligator number thirty-nine somehow missed the train and was later found wallowing in a creek at the foot of Gilmore Street. Number thirty-nine was officially pardoned and sent to the city zoo. The elusive reptile took his place alongside Joe and Old Ocklawaha as one of the legendary three gators of Jacksonville. No longer would they fill streetcars, omnibuses and ferries with happy visitors, but they lived on in spirit to inspire a college football classic, the Gator Bowl.

3

THE DEVIL'S BROTHER

Just as the stately hotels and resorts were ready to cash in on the flood of visitors, the city was dealt the first of five economic setbacks from which it never fully recovered. The first of these was delivered by a tiny apocalyptic mosquito called *Aedes aegypti*. Yellow fever, fire, influenza, loss of the motion picture industry and *theft* of the streetcar system itself did irreparable damage.

On July 28, 1888, R.D. McCormick, visiting the city from Tampa, was admitted to the hospital with "Yellow Jack," commonly known as yellow fever. The doctors assured everyone that it was just an isolated case, and the party continued for a few more days. Then, on August 8, four more cases were admitted, five on the day after that, followed by three the next and so it went until the city was quarantined.

By the end of the epidemic, the vicious Yellow Jack had claimed the lives of over four thousand people, including the mayor of Jacksonville. Needless to say, these conditions staggered the street railways, but under Henry Plant and S.B. Hubbard, Jacksonville's streetcars were financially safe. In an effort to prevent a broader outbreak of yellow fever, the streetcar companies were forbidden from repairing their track, lest they stir up the "sick soil."

Jacksonville was losing its mojo, and Mother Nature was determined to pile on. On August 24, 1885, the city was brushed by a category-two hurricane packing 105-mile-per-hour winds, followed by others that affected the city in 1888, twice in 1893, 1894, 1896 and 1898. During this era of angry winds, the railroads built the huge train shed over the tracks at the Union Depot. The shed was about a city block wide and as long as three football fields; needless to say, it was blown to atoms before it was ever completed. It

was then reconstructed and blown to atoms a second time, but this time the railroads got wise to Mother Nature and put up "butterfly sheds" over each platform rather than an open-ended "zeppelin hangar"–type building. The tropical storms kept coming—we were hit again in 1900, 1906, 1907, 1910, 1914, 1915 and, finally, in 1916. If history teaches us anything in Florida, it's that anyone who bets his or her fortune that Jacksonville is immune to hurricanes is a damned fool.

When news of Frank Sprague's experiment with electric-powered trolleys in Richmond, Virginia, swept across the land, Jacksonville was caught up in "electric fever." The Main Street Railway was the first to string electric wire and bring in the new era of clean transport to Jacksonville. On February 24, 1893, the first electric streetcar in Florida rolled up Main Street from Bay to the former Sub-Tropical Expo grounds at the Municipal Waterworks at First and Main.[6] By March, the entire Main Street Railway was ready for electric service, and the cars were running up Main and around the Walnut Street loop on ten-minute headways.

After a contentious election for which the militia had to be called out, Jacksonville laid down its first pavement. Brick went down on Bay Street from Bridge (Broad) to Market and on Main Street from Bay to Hogan's Creek. Both streets were streetcar routes, and according to the city ordinances, the companies were responsible for paving their track out to six inches on either side.

The success of the electric trolleys and the *clop, clop* of horses and mules on brick pavements brought an immediate attack from the Jacksonville Humane Society, insisting all of the car lines quit using mules in transit service. The modernists on Main Street had upstaged the larger Jacksonville Street Railway and its powerful financial backers with electricity.

In 1893, the Plant System of Railways and Steamships; the Florida Central and Peninsular Railway and the Jacksonville, St. Augustine and Indian River Railway purposed to build a grand union terminal station. The Jacksonville

Opposite, top: The friendly traffic cop signals a horse and wagon across as this big Murray Hill Turtleback loads passengers near Bay and Hogan Streets. *Courtesy of the Jacksonville Historical Society.*

Opposite, bottom: Car 61 appears to be one of the many cars built by the John Stephenson Car Company in New York. Stephenson invented the omnibus on rails that would become the streetcar in 1832 and went on to build tens of thousands of cars prior to being bought out by Brill in 1904. *Courtesy of the Jacksonville Historical Society.*

The massive 1919 Jacksonville Terminal was a busy construction site just beyond the old Union Station, as a large double-truck car pauses for passengers on Bay Street about 1915. *Courtesy of the Library of Congress.*

Terminal Company was chartered with $1 million in capital. The new company's officers read like a "who's who" of southeastern railroading: Duval, Plant, Flagler, Parrott, etc. The Terminal Company was a ready-made traffic and development generator for the streetcar lines. Averaging 20,000 daily passengers for seventy-nine years, the station was the economic life of the streetcars and the city. As of this writing in 2014, Jacksonville International Airport handles about 5,500 passengers fewer passengers per day then the grand old railroad station.

By February, over thirty miles of wire were in place for the installation of incandescent streetlights and electric cars. A bit later the same month, a trainload of new electric streetcars arrived for the Jacksonville Street Railway. On the night of February 28, 1895, the cars were test run up and back to make sure everything worked according to plan. Early the next morning, nine new electric cars clattered out of the barn for the streets of Jacksonville. The first revenue trips were made on March 1, 1895.

The Jacksonville Wheelmen bicycle association proposed building a bicycle-friendly facility at Panama Park. Officials took a long ride out to the site. Upon arrival, the group showed D.F. Jack, president of the Jacksonville Street Railway, around the facility and explained the plans in detail. "We plan to build the finest concrete bike racetrack in the south here," said Mr. Pride, president of the Wheelmen. The group also toured the new casino site, saltwater bathing area, baseball fields, tennis courts, children's playground and the rest of the resort in general.

Mr. Jack committed that the Jacksonville Street Railway would extend its lines out to Panama Park if the Wheelmen continued their own commitment to the project. On that point, there was no doubt—over half of the bonds for the parks construction had already been subscribed.

Pride was more than pleased; he stated, "All that was needed was the certainty of having an electric road from the city to Panama; now that we are assured of having the road built, you can safely say that the Wheelmen will carry out their original plan."

In July, the Main Street Railway ordered a new batch of electric streetcars. They were small, being only twenty-four feet long, and the woodwork in them was said to have made them beauties. On March 1, 1895, the city had eight electric cars on hand with four more expected at any moment.

About this same time, the Jacksonville Street Railway was at work stringing power lines along Bay Street. An issue arose over the city's new power plant. In a statement to the city council, a company representative asked if it could provide power to either public or private locations. The JSRY was making inroads into the power business; already, Union Station and the cooling fans at E.A. Ricker's bought their electricity from the street railway. There was no immediate decision.

It is unclear if the Jacksonville Streetcar System had a dedicated funeral car. In the days before the thirty-automobile motorcades, the venerable funeral car provided the needed space. Generally, a decorated church chapel, complete with stained glass and dark curtains, a party of fifty or so mourners plus a small podium or pulpit and a space for the casket of the deceased would have been provided.

By April 1895, the *Times-Union* was certainly clamoring for such an accommodation. The paper found it strange that though the two lines reached within a mile and a quarter of Evergreen Cemetery, neither had been extended to the "city of the dead."

By August, the Jacksonville Street Railway had reached the Panama Park resort and bicycle track.

In an age before adaptive reuse became common, the beautiful power plant of the Jacksonville Traction Company was unfortunately razed for the Florida Times-Union Newspaper building. *Courtesy of the Florida State Photographic Archives.*

In October, new streetcar ordinances were approved, signed by the mayor and published. The companies were scrambling to get into immediate compliance, though they had strenuously objected to a provision that required two persons—a motorman and a conductor—to be aboard every operating car. The Jacksonville electric railways had presented a case that said it cost the company an additional $6.25 in daily operating expenses and, just to meet this demand, meant that 125 extra passengers a day must board the cars.

On another point, there were loud objections to the placement of a flagman at the corner of Bridge (Broad) and Bay Street. While everyone agreed that this particular intersection was dangerous and it may save lives, the bottom line was that it was going to add two dollars a day, requiring another forty new passengers for the cost of doing business.

The streetcar companies were also being mandated to equip all cars with fenders, an expensive innovation patented just two years before. To the novice, a streetcar fender looks something like a cross between a traditional cowcatcher and a cargo net. Car fenders were quite remarkable—they basically all worked something like this: the large "fender net" sticking out in front of the car was just inches off of the pavement. Stepping into the cars' path, the fenders will knock a person off of their feet and into the net. Weight in the net causes a metal guard to fall across the width of the car under the net and in front of the wheels. As the technology advanced, things such as automatic braking and power cutoff were also possible, without a microchip involved anywhere in the process.

Speed limits were set at eight miles per hour on Bay Street between Market and Bridge (Broad) and on Bridge Street from Bay to Adams as well as Main Street from Bay to Hogan's Creek. Other routes were allowed to speed along at twelve miles per hour, a provision that actually slowed the system down, causing some outcry from the suburban workaday public. For the record, a slow trolley is a misconception, if the cars were presented with the track and the space, they were quite capable of higher speeds. Streetcar variants on the Cincinnati and Lake Erie interurban railway operated up to one hundred miles per hour.

The familiar *clang, clang, clang* of the trolley gong would become a part of the fabric of Jacksonville for the next forty years. A new ordinance required motormen on the cars to sound the gong continuously whenever coming into intersections and passing from one street to another at a speed greater than three miles per hour.

In 1896, electric cars were being assigned all around the city. Open cars toured "the Row" along Riverside Avenue to Edison Avenue during the spring, summer and autumn seasons.

Four electric cars were assigned the Riverside–Fairfield Line, two more on the Market Street–Depot Line, two on the LaVilla–Oakland route and one covered Hogan Street schedules. By May, the final horse car made its trip into Jacksonville history.

Open car number 82 from Oakland meets and passes car 61. *Courtesy of the Jacksonville Historical Society.*

The Main Street Railway ordered two more electric cars in July.

The United States declared war on Spain on April 23. By August 7, 1898, the JSRY had completed an extension of its line to the United States Army camp Cuba Libre in Fairfield. Some twenty-nine thousand young soldiers were scattered in three concentrations—at Fairfield, Panama Park and along Ionia in East Springfield. These men provided the manpower for the Commissary Corps of the United States Seventh Army. Peace was declared on August 13, 1898, and what little soldiering was still done in Jacksonville mounted up and bugged out for Savannah.

The day after peace was declared, the Jacksonville Street Railway announced that it would stop on the far side of all street corners and in the middle of the blocks on Bay Street; this was in keeping with the new city ordinances for the operating companies. On September 9, the company announced that destination signs were installed on all of their cars, one on each end and one on each side.

Jacksonville's Street Railway suffered a setback of untold dimensions when Henry B. Plant died. Shortly after his death, the competing Main Street Railway Company received a thirty-year charter from the City of

Jacksonville. The Main Street Railway also attracted the attention of the Plant System Companies and the media as it received two more electric cars from Pittsburgh.

The newspapers launched a campaign to expand the paved roadway network. With headlines like "Good Roads Pay," the media was pitching a line that these *free* roads would increase the pleasure of the citizens and the profit of their businesses. There was little doubt that roads could amplify business, but that roads amplify business free of charge was an idea that set the course for eventual disaster.

Meanwhile, another storm was brewing over the City of Jacksonville—the landmark United States Supreme Court case *Plessy v. Ferguson*. Many today do not realize that segregation was not universally acceptable in the south. In fact, the railroads and street railways throughout the land were complaining bitterly about the Jim Crow laws. To hold to the letter of the law, the transportation companies would in most cases be required to have two complete sets of equipment to serve every schedule, so even if social justice may not have been the root of the railway argument, the cost implications alone were astronomical.

Jim Crow wasn't exclusively a southern phenomenon; it was taking place in more than half of all states. California, Arizona, Oregon, Connecticut, Maryland, Colorado, Pennsylvania, Ohio, North and South Dakota and many others had similar laws. Swimming upstream, Jacksonville generally ignored the laws; "Jacksonville is regarded by Colored People all over the country as the most liberal town in the South."[7] A full 57 percent of Jacksonville's twenty-eight thousand people in 1900 were Americans of black African decent. So when the city finally got around to falling in line with the state's law, it brought immediate action. Civil rights leaders leaped onto the boycott bandwagon. There was some isolated violence; streetcar crews were threatened, and some sporadic gunfire erupted. The street railways were in a classic Catch-22 situation: while they opposed the segregation, they desperately needed the revenue. They could ignore the law at the risk of losing their franchise or obey it and lose their ridership. They steadfastly refused to empower their conductors with a legal right to determine the race of a passenger. The battle seesawed back and forth for several years. When the boycott weakened because black gentlemen needed to get to work, the city's black women rallied and suggested a general boycott of the city's black men—certainly a move that got everyone's attention.

May 3, 1901, brought the second severe setback to this liberal southern anomaly called Jacksonville. While the City of Angels on America's west

In eight hours, the Great Jacksonville Fire burned 146 city blocks, destroyed more than 2,368 buildings, left ten thousand homeless and devastated Jacksonville. *Courtesy of the Jacksonville Historical Society.*

coast had now topped the one hundred thousand mark, the twenty-eight thousand quirky Jaxsons were about to be staggered with the third most destructive urban fire in United States history.

It all started with a lunch-hour kitchen fire in the Cleveland Mattress Factory. By the time the fire department got on the scene, the conflagration was already moving into surrounding buildings. Thermal updrafts increased the wind velocity, and the fire began to feed itself. Burning embers started drifting back down from the palls of smoke onto the dry rooftops of buildings blocks away. Calls started pouring in about other fires breaking out in the vicinity. By 8:30 p.m. when the fire had reached Hogan's Creek, over 140 city blocks lay in ashes, seven people were dead, ten thousand were homeless and 2,368 buildings were burned to ashes. The governor declared martial law, and the state militia was sent in to assist with rescue and recovery.

Like the rest of the city, the street railways suffered huge financial setbacks. Cars, structures, poles and wires throughout the entire 140-block core were burned, their smoldering remains lying in the streets. Streetcars that were in town when the blaze cut the transmission lines between the Brooklyn and the Main Street generating stations rolled to a stop as their passengers scrambled for safety. The Main Street Railway lost their general offices. Providence smiled on Jacksonville's streetcars as either Hogan's or McCoy's Creek separated the power plants from the conflagration. Likewise, the offices and carbarns of the Jacksonville Street Railway in Brooklyn were spared, along with the rail yard and equipment that was sitting on it. Over on the Main Street Railway, the carbarns near the corner of Eighth and Main were also spared.

Before the embers were cool, New York City was already hard at work raising relief supplies, materiel and cash; ironically, a bond sealed by the blood of war now existed between the two cities.

Perhaps the greatest gift shared with the destitute citizens of Jacksonville was the architect Henry John Klutho. The gifted designer closed down his New York projects and moved to Jacksonville. Within months, he was commissioned to design a new city hall and countless other buildings and public spaces. The influence of this gentleman can scarcely be missed in downtown Jacksonville. In fact, Jacksonville has more examples of the Prairie School style than any city outside the Midwest. Prairie School is a late nineteenth and early twentieth century architectural style, most common to the Midwest. The style is marked by horizontal lines and flat roofs with broad overhanging eaves.

An oddity in the American South is that the railroads were usually built to five-foot or five-foot two-inch gauges, whereas standard-gauge track is four feet eight and a half inches. The Main Street Line was the only standard-gauge operation then in the city, having been standard gauged by franchise requirement, but when the Plant Company finally bought control, it was regauged from standard to the Jacksonville Street Railway's own five-foot gauge, a project that was completed in early 1901.

In spite of the incogitable hardships of the post-fire city, the streetcar companies both enjoyed modest expansions. The Jacksonville Street Railway extended its line from the black picnic grounds at Five Points Swamp to Willow Branch. The Main Street Railway completed its line to Phenix Park, in northeast Jacksonville. Phenix Park was developed as a trolley park, an early-day version of today's Florida theme parks. The wife of the company president suggested the name for Phenix Park; Mrs. F.O. Brown said she wanted it to remain a symbol of the city that rose from the ashes.

Shortly after the fire, the issue of racial segregation flared up again. Being the state's premier city meant that the city of Jacksonville would be the first to feel the bite of the insanity of the Jim Crow era.

After the Great Jacksonville Fire, thousands of unemployed and impoverished migrants flooded into the city looking for work in the reconstruction. Tensions mounted between the citizens and newcomers, coming to a head one evening in June when shots rang out from an unknown assailant, penetrating a streetcar and killing a young black boy. Race riots erupted throughout the metropolitan area until, in desperation, the city council introduced a bill to separate the races.

The segregation ordinance became law in November 1901, six months out from the spark that set Jacksonville's world afire. Two black city councilmen hotly opposed the new law. The gentlemen felt it wasn't needed and suggested clamping down on the new immigrants instead.

Mayor Fletcher signed the law, and ethnicity would continue to be an issue as the street railway conductors were authorized with police powers to determine race and act accordingly, but in reality, this would have affected the bottom line in negative ways by alienating half of the population.

When Stone and Webster bought into the Jacksonville streetcar operations, George Baldwin, a regional manager for the firm out of Savannah, quietly hired the law firm of Judson Douglas Wetmore and James Weldon Johnson of Jacksonville, two of the preeminent attorneys from America's black communities. The law firm worked for the Jacksonville Electric Company in secret to undermine any potential protest. Using Wetmore's advice on the matter, Baldwin instructed all conductors to adhere to the segregation ordinance by keeping silent, emphatically refusing to enforce the law. No longer would blacks be directed to the back of the car or whites to the front; the conductors had their marching orders, and they specified only that they try and seat passengers of like races together or in adjoining seats with the utmost courtesy.

As of 1902, construction was everywhere—a new city of stone, mortar and steel.

JACKSONVILLE ELECTRIC COMPANY

With Henry Plant gone, the Plant System Companies were rather rapidly sold off or reorganized. The Jacksonville Street Railway, the Main Street Railroad and the Jacksonville Electric Light Company were consolidated into the new Jacksonville Electric Company, with C.A. Stone and E.S. Webster on the board.

Downtown Jacksonville is where Florida happened for the first one hundred years after statehood. This scene shows one of a sizable fleet of four-wheel open cars unopposed on otherwise busy streets. *Courtesy of the Library of Congress.*

The fifteen-mile railway and utility company was capitalized at $1 million with stock subscription. The first mortgage was $1,250,000 due in gold on May 1, 1927.

4
ANOTHER FINE MESS

NORTH JACKSONVILLE STREET RAILWAY TOWN AND IMPROVEMENT COMPANY

On March 11, 1903, Jacksonville made national news again when the press released word that a contract was awarded to D.M. Baker, a Jacksonville resident, for construction of the "North Springfield Street Railway,"[8] a wholly owned black enterprise built to the highest standards.

R.R. Robinson and a group of prominent citizens from Jacksonville's flourishing black community were awarded a franchise to link the northwest side of town with the rest of the street railway network and business core on July 1, 1902. With enthusiastic buy-in from the community, the North Jacksonville Street Railway, Town and Improvement Company gained national attention as the "Colored Man's Railroad." The board of directors included R.R. Robinson, Walter P. Mucklow, George E. Ross, H. Mason, F.C. Eleves and Frank P. McDermott. The road was to extend four miles, commencing at Clay and Bay Streets and running north on Clay to State to Kings to the city limits on Durkee Shell Road (present-day Myrtle Avenue). Ultimately, the company would loop back along Thirteenth Street east to Moncrief and south on Davis through Hansontown.

Work on the NJSRYT&IC had been roaring along. Track work was complete on July 10, and the company was busy stringing wires. The city, if

For the most part, the beautiful brick streets, some of the church steeples and all of the small four-wheeled Stephenson Cars built for the Jacksonville Electric Company are lost. *Courtesy of the Jacksonville Historical Society.*

not the whole nation, was anxiously waiting for the first of the new electric cars to arrive. *Railway Age Magazine* wrote a description of the new railroad with no small amount of amazement that a black community, especially in the Deep South, could accomplish such a feat.

The NJSRYT&IC established North Jacksonville Park at the northeast corner of Myrtle and Thirteenth Streets; the park's name was soon changed to Mason's Park and then again to Roosevelt Park. This park included the company's general offices and carbarn. No expenses were being spared, and Mason's Park had a handsome dance and concert hall. More amenities were added over the next few years.

Nearly one year later, in May 1903, the city council awarded the company a franchise to expand, allowing it to build east on State to Washington to Jessie Street in Oakland, with a line that ended at Talleyrand Avenue in the port area. Thus, the new road would connect two unattached and primarily black business and residential districts, one northwest and the other northeast of downtown. It seemed surreal that black citizens could now ride their own electric railway. Amazingly, the cars were segregated. Black passengers rode in front, and the white passengers rode in the rear; this was after all, following the letter of the law.

The opening of the new road was attended by a great host of people of all races. The opening included a vast picnic, filled with music and promising speeches by mayor George M. Nolan, former mayor Duncan U. Fletcher and many others.

ATLANTIC AND PACIFIC STREET RAILWAY AND SECURITIES COMPANY

The directors could not agree on how to market the shares in the company. Robinson wanted them freely available on the open market, and the others leaned toward a closed-stock model. The franchise stipulated that the line be complete in one year, but owing to financial difficulties, the city granted an extension until May 1, 1905. Robinson incorporated the Atlantic and Pacific Street Railway and Securities Company in New Jersey to take over and complete the railroad, but his attempt failed.

By the end of February 1905, an application was filed for the court to appoint a receiver to the NJSRYT&IC. Judgments and liens against the property totaled over $2,500. While the company itself claimed it was the cost of electrical power and the contribution to the city that cost them profitability, others claimed mismanagement and failure to adhere to the letter of the franchise.

The company was not running four cars daily as per the franchise; it was simply running one. The other three cars were sidetracked, broken and out of service. As a result, the published schedules could not be maintained, nor could taxes be paid.

A discharge was levied by the Seaboard Airline Railway, stating the company had failed to install a physical lockout device known as a derailer where it crossed the Seaboard. An injunction was issued restraining the company from incurring any new debit, and it was ordered liquidated.

Ultimately, the company was sold to the developer Telfair Stockton and Associates. Stockton would be able to easily complete the construction mandated in the franchise making the new road 6.4 miles in length but removed its unique status as a black enterprise.

Stockton was about to find out that this was not going to be a cakewalk and that achieving that illusionary panacea of the "ever-profitable" electric railway was easier said than done.

ᴺORTH ᴶACKSONVILLE ᴼTREET ᴿAILWAY

To prevent utter confusion on the issue, it should be explained that Telfair Stockton's proposed North Jacksonville Street Railway was a completely different project than his newly purchased NJSRYT&IC. The older NJSRYT&IC already had a franchise to reach Talleyrand Avenue in Jacksonville's eastside harbor district. Once completed, the railway would form a single line from Jacksonville's northwest to the east side, skirting the northern edge of the downtown core.

The ensuing drama was over Stockton's new North Jacksonville Street Railway. No doubt the intention was to build the new railway, eventually merge in the older NJSRYT&IC and then, if municipal ownership was decided upon, sell the whole thing to the city at some profit. In fact, Stockton referred to such a possibility several times in the heated city council debates.

A passenger detrains at the rear of the large open car 91 as another passenger rides the rear platform. The car is on the Fairfield–Depot Line but it advertises the Phoenix Park Line, "Direct to the Ostrich Farm." Sharp-eyed readers might notice the knotted side curtains on the open car. The closed number 110 car is on the First and Walnut Line. *Courtesy of the Jacksonville Historical Society.*

In a conference held by the city council on January 5, 1905, strong opposition was voiced over the new North Jacksonville Streetcar Company now being promoted by Telfair Stockton. Somewhat an anomaly for that era, councilmen and large collection of citizens explained their opposition. When the council invited the promoters to explain their project, Telfair Stockton replied that he would rather hear the objections before responding.

Councilman Blair could not understand why the proposed Riverside Line could not go in back of Riverside Park, rather than in front of it. Stockton replied that the company's object was to go where houses, people and businesses were. Stockton said he wanted to help the people and the city but that the company needed to make something out of it.

Councilman Bowden wanted the company to post a bond and pay the city 2 percent of its gross income. Councilman Cockrell then piled on, stating that 2 percent was not enough and 3 to 5 percent was more realistic. He said our schoolchildren should be remembered, and no child should pay full fare. The councilman stood firmly against any potential competition to the city's electric light plant, as well as any new streetcar line using Laura, Duval and Park Streets.

Councilman Cooper joined the battle: he thought that in spite of highly successful "trolley tours," no street used as a scenic driveway in such a tourist-dominated city should be *marred* by a street railway. He reiterated his belief that streetcars crossing the Duval Street Viaduct would be damaging and dangerous. He also had an aversion to any new wires being strung in the city. The modern reader should understand, however, that his argument was not aimed solely at electric street railways; in those days, every telephone required an individual wire, and electricity distribution was equally primitive. For every four- to eight-wire electric transmission or telephone pole in the city today, fifty to one hundred wires would have existed.

By January 9, the primary objections boiled down to tracks on certain streets. Forsyth, Laura, Park and Duval Streets were apparently forbidden. The principal reason for this was the fact that Bay Street was already the primary east–west streetcar thoroughfare, while the hacks, stages and buggies primarily used these alternative streets.

On February 1, *Jacksonville Metropolis* offered hope that the city was once more forging ahead. All eyes were now on the municipal ownership of Jacksonville's streetcar system. People were convinced that street railways were so profitable that municipal ownership would slash their taxes. The reporters were told that the council was elected on a platform of municipal ownership of utilities and infrastructure: "Just wait until Tuesday, and you will see if we are true to our word."

On February 4, the headlines announced: "Rejected" and "Jacksonville Should Own the Streetcar Lines." Arguments were reiterated as reasons for the rejection, but perhaps the most significant was commonsensical. With the exception of two lines, every route of the proposed North Jacksonville Muni (assuming it became municipal) was parallel to and competitive with the Jacksonville Electric Company's established routes.

The committee had to either reject municipal ownership and Stockton's new franchise application or approve Stockton in favor of the city eventually owning the railways. Yet approving Stockton's franchise and growing an enormous system would have guaranteed that municipal ownership would be beyond the city's abilities and financially impossible.

By the end of February, the whole city council met as a committee to further discuss Stockton's proposal. Stockton said he understood that the committee to whom it was referred had killed the idea, but then he was informed that only the proposed bill for a new ordinance was postponed indefinitely.

Stockton, a well-known developer and man of great means, said he and his associates were ready, willing and most able to start construction on tracks just as soon as the proposal was approved. He said that they could complete two-thirds of the project within two years from the date of the council's approval and that he was willing to give a bond of assurance to the city to that effect. "We are all well-known citizens of Jacksonville and are financially able to build, equip and operate the road. We can meet any reasonable proposition of the city, the council or the proposed amendments."

Stockton's final words in this all-important meeting were to place the whole thing in the hands of the voters, no doubt at his expense: "Let them decide this for themselves. And as for municipal ownership, there was no one and no group of associates more in favor of the idea then we are, but we all know that is simply not practical at this time." Stockton then focused all of his energies on expanding on his NJSRYT&IC railway.

Councilman R.F. Bowden said he would move to have the promoters post the bond and submit it to the council.

The city recorder then read the bill into the record and various members then proposed the amendments. In the end, it was decided that the proposed road commence using Catherine Street rather than Liberty, Oak rather than Park, Margaret instead of Francis, Ashley instead of Church, Adams instead of East Duval, Cedar (today's Pearl) instead of Laura (downtown) and, finally, Silver instead of Pearl (in Springfield).

On March 15, 1905, the evening *Jacksonville Metropolis* published a remarkable editorial explaining the benefits of streetcars, an editorial that is just as valid in the twenty-first century as it was then.

THEY ARE DEVELOPERS

It is to be hoped now that the new owners of the North Jacksonville Street Railway will improve the property and make it a developer, as has been always characteristic of the present Jacksonville Electric Company's railroad. There is probably not another thing that can rightfully claim to have done as much or more than the latter company in expanding territory and enhancing values in this city. This magnificent and well-managed road penetrates nearly every section of the city, and assists materially in building up along its lines in a most remarkable manner. One of the causes of the popularity of the road is that all patrons can have passage in the city from one end

The downtown loops at the foot of Main Street made sense when downtown was the place to be. *From the author's collection.*

to the other of the lines for five cents. A change of routes carries no additional charge to the patron.

What were old abandoned fields and scrubs a few years ago have been transformed by this road into lots, blocks and streets, and are now important parts of the city proper. We have never thought that street railroads did any harm to a city, but instead were beneficial to it. The proposition is to build an entirely new railroad here, and with the two other roads now in operation Jacksonville should grow very fast in valuable territory and population. There are few men, including the chronic kicker, but what would deeply regret to see the railroads suspend operations even for one day. The Electric Company's road has proven true and equal to every demand. It has kept up its service through calamities as well as at all other times, day and night, improving its equipment for the benefit of patrons and enlarging its sphere of usefulness in every way possible. Now, as a change has been made in the ownership of one run down road, and the proposition is made for rights to build another the three should give the city the best service in the South and push Atlanta close as the most enterprising city of the South.

There was no doubt that the North Jacksonville Line was serious business, no boodlers involved, and that the great debate would continue to rage until all parties were satisfied.

The "North Jacksonville Street Railway," proposal and the "North Jacksonville Street Railway Town and Improvement Company," continued, understandably, to confuse the press. In short, the new franchise was not about to be approved without amendments, as several of the routes were within one block of one another.

The older NJSRYT&IC already had a right to expand into the east side, which would prove a lucrative source of revenue. Materials for that extension were due to arrive shortly. Along with rail, ties, spikes, poles, wires and electrical substations, streetcars of the newest design had been ordered. Stockton intended to be conspicuous and pique the city council's curiosity, challenging its interest. The new extension of the NJSRT&I Company would start at the connection with its tracks at the corner of Clay and State Streets, run on streets "still to be decided upon," thence east through East Jacksonville to Talleyrand Avenue. That decision ultimately became Washington to Union, Union to Florida, Florida to Duval, Duval to Parker, Parker to Marshall and Marshall to the end of the line at Talleyrand. Stockton said the new Eastside Line would be completed by May 1, 1905, at which time it would be put into full operation.

Among the other changes to the North Jacksonville Street, Railway Town and Improvement Company, Stockton changed the name of Mason's Park to Roosevelt Park. Stockton thought the new name would be pleasing to "colored people," who were the main patrons of line. Around the same time as the name change, Telfair Stockton was elected president and general manager of the road, Sam Holmes was elected secretary and Ernest C. Bud was selected as treasurer.

5
THE BATTLE OF THE CENTURY

Word spread across the city that a municipal league would be formed to push for city ownership of the streetcar system and all other utilities. The league planned to suggest that the municipal ownership question could be settled at the ballot box. Telfair Stockton himself was convinced that with municipal ownership of the electric plant, water plant, and streetcar system, the city would have so much income it would no longer need to tax the citizens at all.

The new North Jacksonville Street Railway men firmly believed in municipal ownership of all city utilities. But they also believed that the city was nowhere near able to build and manage such an enterprise, should the council approve it and send it to the voters. Meanwhile, they reiterated their promise to build the new street railway on the alternative streets suggested, and they would post a large pond to ensure its completion. Certainly these men could post as large a bond as the city council could imagine.

In the event city council decided to put the new street railway before the voters, all of the stipulations could be plainly stated on the ballot. With all of the amendments added, it would be up to the people of the city to either accept or reject the new railway.

On March 6, 1905, the evening *Metropolis* reported that the city council committee on ordinances and rules would soon hold a hearing on the question. People on both sides of the issue were invited to speak up; overall, the entire city was for the new street railway with the single exception of Riverside. The balance of the city knew for certain that the new street

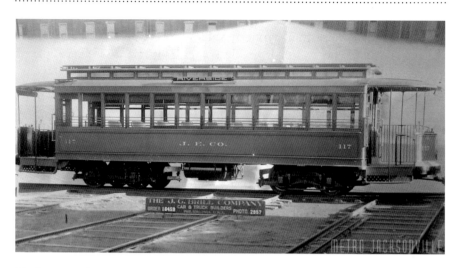

The long-term loyalty of the First Coast street railways to the John Stephenson Car Company didn't vanish when Brill purchased the firm in 1904. These Brill cars featured clerestory windows that tilted out for ventilation. *Courtesy of metrojacksonville.com.*

Behold the interior of a real trolley. Have you ever had the joy of riding in one of those glorified potato chip trucks that run around towns posing as faux trolleys? Hard wooden seats typify the fakes, along with faux brass–plated plastic, cheap plywood and a life span of eight years. *Courtesy of metrojacksonville.com.*

railway would increase their property values and create new development. New development beyond their stately homes is exactly what the people of Riverside did not want.

In Memphis, *News-Scimitar* protested the municipal ownership of the car lines in that city because it "reeked of socialism." In Jacksonville, however, it appeared in the city that the municipal ownership group would steamroll the issue and crush the opposition.

Streetcar companies were riding an all-time high, no other industry in America could provide such returns; it appeared the industry was untouchable.

Whatever came of the Jacksonville Municipal League proposal, they were certain to cite examples in municipal ownership. Chicago's success in municipal ownership of that city utilities suggested that municipal ownership of the streetcars would only improve what was perceived as poor service. Jacksonville's embryonic municipal league apparently thought forming a Jacksonville Transportation Authority could only improve on streetcars and twelve-minute headways.

The debate over municipal ownership devolved into a full-scale war. On May 30, 1905, bold headlines in the *Jacksonville Metropolis* stated, "P.A. Holt's Efforts to Humbug People." The article warned against Mr. Holt's machinations, saying he was the "enemy of municipal ownership."

"Holt, with certain other men, is making a desperate effort to get control of the city of Jacksonville. A dark day for the city if the plan succeeds, official record of Holt and Dodge during the time the question of extending the Jacksonville Electric Company's franchise came up before the council. Councilman Rinehart unmasks the designs of Holt, a scathing arrangement.

Holt and Dodge at the last meeting of the city Council, without consultation with Mr. Betts, Reported back to the council adversely; two ordinances, one favoring the submission to the voters of all Ordinances Granting Street Railway and other municipal franchises, and the other authorizing the use of profits of the electric plant to increase the capability of that plant, and that they submitted with that report legal briefs on the subjects, which would make any lawyer, not a paid opponent of municipal ownership, laugh with derision.

But for the sadness of the spectacle of two councilmen chosen by the city electors to represent them and protect their interest so betraying the city's electric light plant interests.

It should be borne in mind that the committee on laws is referred to with every ordinance introduced into the city council, and that they have a very great influence over all municipal legislations, and that this committee consists of three members the president, Mr. Dodge and Mr. Betts, the last two appointed. While Mr. Barrett's is in thorough accord with the friends of the electric plant and municipal ownership generally, Mr. Holt and Dodge consistently act together as though opposed there to, and that the only way to change the committee by laws and rules so as to be in harmony with what I consider necessary to protect the city's interest is to change the president of the Council and ask if Mr. Betts a fellow member of that committee favorable to meet us for ownership and opposed to granting franchises for electric plants or granting franchises without the vote of the electors."

With excitement over Telfair Stockton's new North Jacksonville Street Railway still running at fever pitch, residents of Riverside presented a petition to the Jacksonville Electric Railway to extend a line southward to the city limits.

The fender issue reappeared frequently in the back and forth between the electric railways and the City of Jacksonville. Apparently, some early version was used, but there was never a satisfactory solution found on the fender mandate of 1895; ten years later, it came up for discussion again. On March 31, the board of public works discussed another plan to require fenders on all cars.

When the new Jacksonville Electric Company franchise was approved, it stipulated that the company would be required to provide free transfers. A further burden was levied on the company beyond paying taxes and paving streets. The new franchise also assessed the company 3 percent of all fares collected rising to 5 percent after five years.

Despite ballooning expenses, the Jacksonville Electric Company under Stone and Webster management had already laid out some $200,000 in local spending. A new $50,000 general office building for the company was ready for occupancy by the end of June.

The railway soon received its first two new, larger double-motor trolleys. One was immediately employed on the long picturesque Phenix Park line; the other was employed running from Fairfield through downtown and south into Riverside.

Manager Tucker of the Jacksonville Electric Company Railway explained to the board of public works that the streetcar company would be double tracking Main Street. This news was exceptionally well received by the anxious residents of Springfield as it promised to speed service.

On May 17, 1904, the Jacksonville Electric Company would be requested to take up the streetcar tracks running from the main line on Main Street to the old carbarn near Eighth Street.

July 1904 was a busy month for the railways of Jacksonville. Once again the "fender problem" raised its ugly head. Chairman Peter A. Dignan of the board of public works had once again demonstrated to the board that there was a city ordinance requiring fenders on the cars. The Jacksonville Electric Company shot back that it was up to the board of public works to determine the kind of fender to be used, and so far, that hadn't happened. For the electric company's part, it stated it was more than willing to comply if the board could reach a consensus.

Adding insult to injury, when the board of public works finally went shopping for the preferred fender, it solicited the Providence Fender, which had to be operated by the motorman. Manager Tucker of the Jacksonville Electric Company explained that the Providence Fender required the motorman to operate it and, at the same time, cut the power and brake the car to a stop—this was simply a dangerous action.

Tucker also commented that he was installing a switch and sidetrack at the Jacksonville Opera House on Main Street for the benefit of the many patrons of the new playhouse establishment.

With the winter season crowd packing the hotels, the company placed a new open-air electric car on the Riverside Line. The car was given the number 77, which speaks to the sheer size of the ever-expanding company. This new car was ordered following the precedent set several years before with destination signs on each side and on each end.

A somewhat comical event happened in October. In those days, according to city ordinance, every car was staffed by both a motorman, who actually operated the car, and a conductor, who collected fares, issued transfers and sold tickets and tokens. On this particular day, car 90 made a westbound turn onto Bay from Main Street. As the conductor stood on the steps, his attention was obviously focused on some nearby distraction; car 90 was met by another car going in the opposite direction. He was knocked clear off the car and landed on the street. Not badly injured, he immediately leapt to his feet and regained his position on the steps of car 90. Brushing himself off with the classic line, "There's nothing to see here, folks," he regained charge and reassumed his captaincy.

In November, the Jacksonville Board of Trade, recognizing that the street railway was key to the city's economic growth, met with manager Tucker of the Jacksonville Electric Company with ideas for a series of innovative experiments to improve service on the railway.

Jacksonville's position on the railroad map as the Chicago of Florida, a city growing its station facilities into what was rapidly becoming the undisputed railroad passenger capital of the south, was causing no small amount of alarm as the rail yards expanded westward across Myrtle Avenue. The city's board of public works went on a visit to Savannah, where a similar situation had existed on Gwinnett Street and its Union Station until a subway tunnel corrected it. Chairman Dignan said that much information had been collected. Gwinnett Street Subway was eight hundred feet long, but four hundred feet would meet all of Jacksonville's requirements. Thus the impetus for Florida's first, last and only subway, the Myrtle Avenue Subway in Jacksonville.

In 1905, Jacksonville's terminal station was already comparing favorably with stations in America's major cities. Forty passenger trains arrived and forty passenger trains departed every day, and thousands of people thronged around the station. One railroad official commented, "Once our trains leave New York, they see nothing more of that type of depot and activity until they reach Jacksonville terminal."

A heartbreaking accident occurred one morning on the corner of Adams and Newnan Streets at eleven o'clock. The six-year-old grandson of Jay L. Taylor, of the United States Post Office, was run over by streetcar number 35 of the LaVilla Oakland line. The little boy was riding his bicycle eastward along Bay and did not heed the streetcar's warning; on seeing the little boy, the motorman immediately cut the power and set the brakes. He frantically stomped the pedal that sounded the gong. In the last moment, the little boy saw the streetcar, and it appeared for a second that he was going to make it across the track. He crossed the first rail but at the second rail appeared to try to dismount his bicycle. In his panic, he swerved and the wheel caught the flangeway; he fell off the bike immediately to the side of the streetcar track. The overhang on the car hit him, sending him into violent somersaults. The conductor and motorman were terribly shaken up by the whole incident.

A policeman by the name of Powell was said to have been standing on the corner and saw the whole accident. Powell ran into the street, scooped up the little boy, cradling the child in his arms and sprinted to his home in the Columns, on the corner of Ocean and Forsyth Streets. Dr. J.H. Pitman came immediately to Powell's house and examined the child. The doctor said he was painfully injured and administered morphine. By 1:30 p.m., Mrs. Taylor told gathered good Samaritans that the child was resting peacefully. And now that the child was resting, Powell returned to the streetcar with a vengeance. He immediately arrested conductor U.A. Knight and motorman G.A. Smith for reckless operation of a streetcar. After being booked on the charges, each man was released on fifty dollars bail.

About the same time, the newspapers reported another small boy who tragically encountered a streetcar. And if the people were saddened by the first accident, this one horrified them. Reporters said,

> A little Negro boy, of 1111 State St., was run over by a streetcar of the North Jacksonville Line at the corner of Johnson Street and Kings Road and killed. Two little boys were playing a game of chase when little Lucius Connenient, darted directly in front of the oncoming streetcar. Motorman Henry Chestnut, and his "captain" Conductor Lane, was placed under arrest. The streetcar passed over the little boy's body nearly severing it; the incident was so violent that it derailed the streetcar.

There was an assumption in both of these cases that the streetcars were being operated at excessive speed, violating the city's twelve-miles-per-hour speed limit. The judge exonerated the streetcar men, stating that in these types of occurrences, car operators will do everything in their power to avert such an accident. The justice also said there were sufficient witnesses to prove that the railway crews had absolutely no responsibility in these accidents.

If it wasn't already known, the fact is that railroad tracks, not unlike modern freeways, make terrible playgrounds. So if you take nothing else from this book, please remember that it takes just 4 pounds of pressure to turn a tomato into ketchup, whereas a train can exert 550,000 pounds of force. Streetcar lines are railways; it's as simple as that.

6
THE STOLEN JOOLS

J.C. Tracy made a presentation to the county commissioners for an interurban railway between South Jacksonville and Atlantic Beach. No fewer than four companies would eventually announce a similar intent. As a historian and a retired transportation man, it is my opinion that these roads would have been among the greatest infrastructure projects to ever be built in the City of Jacksonville and the surrounding communities. Some have accused Jacksonville of being "a diamond that wants to remain coal," and the failure, if not the outright theft, of the great interurban roads may have been the first time in our modern history that Jacksonville shot itself in the foot.

Whether the petition of J.C. Tracey was serious is unknown. He apparently had no history in Jacksonville, and no one knew anything of his means. But the interurban proposition was fascinating nonetheless.

High-speed rail is not a new concept in the United States; in fact, we taught the world and then junked our entire network, save .09 percent. It was the interurban networks that blanketed many states with twenty thousand miles of track—much of a high speed. The great interurbans of Charlotte, Atlanta, Dallas and Los Angeles amounted to thousands of miles of luxurious, clean, quiet transportation.

In Jacksonville, there were now proposals for interurbans to Atlantic Beach, another to Pablo Beach and yet another would come along to Jacksonville Beach. One company backed by a millionaire from St. Joseph, Missouri, proposed laying track from Jacksonville to Miami,

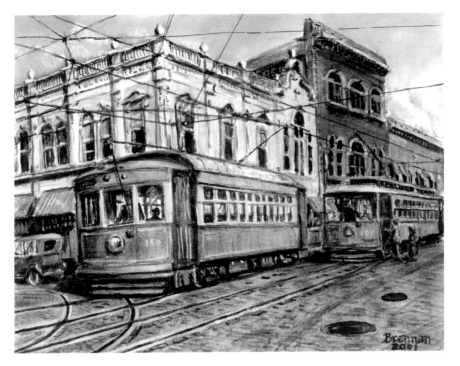

Local artist Larry Brennan captured the color of Jacksonville Traction in this pastel. Larry's art can be found online at http://lpbrennan.deviantart.com. *Courtesy of LP Brennan.*

Daytona to Sanford and another link to Tampa. There was a separate proposal for a line from St. Augustine to Jacksonville via a tunnel under the St. Johns River. A second mainline would run from St. Augustine to Ponte Vedra and on to Jacksonville. In Ocala, an interurban actually started operation and was supposed to terminate in Jacksonville. These were the cases of the "stolen jools."

At least three of these actually started construction, and a fourth was a conceptual interurban, completely in place all the way to Jacksonville Beach and Mayport, but by then, the city had bought into the idea that "rail is not a good fit for Jacksonville."[9] One can only imagine today what a godsend such a silver racetrack would be today.

SILVER SPRINGS AND OCALA ELECTRIC RAILWAY AND THE JACKSONVILLE, OCALA AND SILVER SPRINGS ELECTRIC RAILWAY

Perhaps the earliest of the grand electric proposals was that of the Ocala roads starting in 1896. The conversation in the city had turned to extending a great interurban (today's light rail) between Ocala, Silver Springs and the city of Jacksonville. The citizens of Jacksonville were in discussion over bonding the city to build the new electric line. Surveys for this road were underway by August, and by the eighth of the month, construction was begun on the "Silver Springs and Ocala Electric Railway."

By February 1897, the Jacksonville, Ocala and Silver Springs Electric Railway had operated its first train in Ocala. The electric interurban never reached beyond Silver Springs.

More interurban gains seem to have been made between St. Augustine and Jacksonville as well as Jacksonville Beach and South Jacksonville, where some twelve miles, evenly split between two companies (six miles of each line) were graded. Another five to six miles from downtown to San Jose actually got rail but then stalled. Apparently though, the project was revived by the City of South Jacksonville some five years later.

That Stone and Webster were curious is an understatement; telegrams were flying to and fro. It's clear that the Jacksonville Electric Company would have benefited from the presence of an interurban network, but outside of some track and proposals, it never happened.

JACKSONVILLE SUBURBAN AND SEASHORE

By midsummer 1905, promoters promised a line to the beach. John D. Lawrence was president of the corporation, and William A. Riddle served on the corporate board. Track work was to begin as soon as letters of patent were issued by Governor Broward. The new railway was another interurban project, though its name didn't state as much. Some twenty miles of new line would link Jacksonville, South Jacksonville and Pablo Beach (Jacksonville Beach) according to the plan.

In August 1905, the company announced that track work contracts had been given to the American Railway Construction Company and said construction would commence within sixty days.

The names were familiar; the newspaper trumpeted "fact" that this time it would be different because it appeared to everyone that Lawrence and associates had experience in several significant business deals locally.

Stone and Webster launched an investigation. On closer examination, it turned out that neither man was that "man of means," portrayed by the papers—it was a case of mistaken identity.

JACKSONVILLE FERNANDINA AND SOUTHERN RAILROAD

The company applied for a charter in early 1905 to build a twenty-eight-mile road between Jacksonville and Fernandina. Tied to the timber industry, Samuel A. Swann and William A. Evans, both of Fernandina, incorporated the road.

FLORIDA INTERURBAN RAILWAY AND TUNNEL COMPANY

Incorporated by members of the well-known Bates-Dowling real estate firm, M.W. Bates was to be the president of the company and John Mabry vice-president. Bates was known as "an old railroad man."

Announced on September 18, 1912, the forty-five-mile electric railway would have included a tunnel under the St. Johns River, connecting Jacksonville with South Jacksonville, Pablo Beach and St. Augustine. The tunnel under the river would have been designed for electric railcars, pedestrians and vehicles, thus becoming the first fixed river crossing for local traffic.

ST. AUGUSTINE AND PALATKA RAPID TRANSIT COMPANY

The St. Augustine and Palatka Rapid Transit Company had a capital stock of $2 million and, by May 1913, announced its intent to construct an electric road running parallel to the Florida East Coast Railway, mainline between St. Augustine, Elkton, Vermont Heights, Spuds, Hastings, East Palatka and Palatka. The road would be twenty-six miles in length, and the powerhouse would be located in Hastings. The investors were all capitalists from Washington, D.C. It would connect with St. Augustine's streetcars.

PALATKA-HASTINGS INTERURBAN RAILWAY

The Palatka-Hastings Interurban Railway was a logical interurban proposal that could have served the rich farm belt between its two namesake cities. Though not as ambitious as the St. Augustine and Palatka road, it may have been one of those rare "paper railroads" with a chance of success.

On January 18, 1913, the *Chicago Packer Newspaper* ran an article titled "Road to Tap Spud District; Interurban Railway Planned from Palatka to Hastings." The article spoke well to the fact that while street railways generally focused solely on passenger transportation, interurbans were focused on a traffic mix of passengers, mail, express and freight. "Leading citizens of St. Johns and Putnam Counties have applied for a charter for an interurban railway from Palatka to Hastings, running through the celebrated Hastings potato district."

The Palatka-Hastings Interurban Railroad Company filed on January 13, 1913, and letters of patent were issued on March 18, 1913. The company was based in Palatka.

The *Contractor Magazine* chimed in that the City of Hastings had granted a franchise to the Palatka-Hastings Interurban Railroad, revealing that one C.A. DuPont was the president.

The *Tradesman, Southern Hardware*, Volume 69, understood more about the relationship between fixed-rail infrastructure and urban development in 1913 than the current crop of consultants and planners employed by either the Jacksonville Transportation Authority or the Florida Department of Transportation. Though the writing style is very nineteenth century, the message remains poignantly refreshing.

> As a practical demonstration of the theory of building a city, by building the city-building material at home; or carrying out the idea that men, not cities, were created by all wise Providence-Palatka is developing along prudent, yet progressive lines, producing results far ahead of any of the smaller cities of the state of Florida, or elsewhere for that matter, so far as the writer's

observation extends. Since July, 1913, through the systematic work of the Palatka Board of Trade, the Palatka-Hastings Interurban Railroad-Capital $250,000, the Palatka Development Company, Capital $50,000 have been organized by the citizens of Palatka and her twin sister, Hastings citizens, the most of whom were born and raised in this county.

Howell A. Davis, president of G.M. Davis and Son Manufacturers; president Palatka Development Company; vice president Palatka-Hastings Interurban Railroad; vice president, Palatka Automobile and Supply Company and president of the Palatka Board of Trade, is one demonstration of the development of city-building material. A purely Palatka product, who has associated with him, in the various other enterprises named other Palatka men who have developed into city builders right here at home.

At least, this was the case until the Putnam County Commissioners refused to allow the company to use the long drawbridge linking Palatka with East Palatka. Without the bridge, the project was dead.

Jacksonville and St. Augustine Public Service Company

It was reported in the June 20, 1914 *Electric Railway Journal* that a franchise was granted and the road had completed grading six miles of its proposed forty-mile interurban line south from South Jacksonville. Plans were being made to build a new bridge across the bay from St. Augustine to North Beach. It would run from South Jacksonville to "Beach Junction," Diego, Pablo Beach and St. Augustine. The general manager of the company was Thomas R. Osmond of Jacksonville.

Jacksonville-Middleburg Electric Railway

This was another project that was roaring along by the beginning of 1915. Grading was underway from Jacksonville Heights (centered at today's Old Middleburg Road and 103rd Street) to the Seaboard Lackawanna Shops (old West Jax rail yard) and hence into town. When this section was completed, they planned to move to the Middleburg end of the line and build north to Jacksonville Heights, closing the gap and connecting the two halves. Right of way along the entire twenty-four-mile railway had been secured. The first ten miles had been financed, and material and labor contracts were let. Local residents were contracted to give time, labor and ties, in addition to offering to take stock in the company as soon as organization was complete. Eventually, a steam logging road, the Middleburg, Highland and Lake Butler Railroad, actually served Middleburg for a short time.

Jacksonville, Miami and Tampa Interurban Railway

Kicking off the year 1917 was an interesting proposal, by far the largest interurban idea Jacksonville would ever see. The JM&TI was backed by multimillionaire True Davis, an early pharmaceutical magnet from St. Joseph, Missouri. Davis proposed laying track and stringing wire from Jacksonville to Pablo Beach, St. Augustine, Daytona Beach, Cocoa Beach, Melbourne, Hopkins and on to Miami. The second mainline would have run from Hopkins (today's "south" Melbourne, Florida) west to Haines City, Lakeland, Plant City, Tampa and ultimately Tarpon Springs. Finally a branchline was to have run from Daytona Beach to Sanford, roughly along the current I-4 alignment. Everyone anticipated the railway, but the company abruptly and inexplicitly vaporized.

Jacksonville and Seashore Electric Association

The company was formed in 1917 to continue the dream of connecting the city with the beaches. Though the name sounded similar to the earlier effort, this time the board of directors read like a "who's who" of area businesses. The new company stated that its purpose was to build an electric (interurban) railway between downtown and the beach. M.B. Jennings was elected president; Judge H.B. Philips, W.R. Rannie, Telfair Stockton, P.J. Mundy, E.W. Waybright, F.O. Miller and Sam Marshall, vice-presidents, and St. Elmo W. Acosta was the secretary of the association.

Acosta was able to take a resolution to the capital at Tallahassee to put the issue up for a vote by the people of Duval County. Things were looking good when the state house of representatives passed the measure, but then the state senate allowed it to die. The interests of this group didn't wane, and as late as the early 1930s, it was still attempting to pull together the great interurban road. Sadly, by that time, the city of Jacksonville had sold its soul to General Motors.

7

HOLLYWOOD PARTY

The Jacksonville Electric Company superintendent Tucker announced that it would expend $26,000 for a large improvement project. Many curves were slated for reconstruction, and the rest of the list reads like a primer on railway 101.

New heavy rail and single track on the grass strip along Phelps and First Streets was being installed. New, heavy one-hundred-pounds-to-the-yard rail of the latest type of steel was going down on new curves on First between Main and Market. New construction stretching 1,100 feet on Date (today's Edison Avenue) from Riverside Avenue and the addition of 60 feet of new pavement. From the corner of Main and Phelps Streets, 886 feet of new double track was added, including track over the new concrete bridge over Hogans Creek, which the Jacksonville Electric Company paid for. Over on Florida Avenue (today's A.P. Randolph) 1,400 feet of new heavy-railed track with new brick pavement, plus another 500 feet of new gravel pavement was going in. Newnan Street from Duval northward to Union Street got another 1,080 feet of new track. On Hogan Street, a new 350-foot extension was being hammered home in addition to new curves leading from Hogan to Beaver. All of the curves and switch work in the Oakland neighborhood were getting the new heavy-rail rebuild too.

Coinciding with this, an entirely new line opened on Florida Avenue from end to end, piercing what was one of the most prosperous black business districts in the nation.

Car 148 is about to turn from Main to Bay on its Riverside and Pearl Line, which ran from Eleventh and Pearl to Aberdeen Street in Riverside. In the background, another car turns east to run the Ocean Street Loop shared by the First and Walnut, Kings Road and Oakland Lines. *Courtesy of the Jacksonville Historical Society.*

The Jacksonville Electric Company already had all of the new materials paid for and on hand. The work was being pushed as hard and as fast as the company could move. The city resounded with the songs of the "gandy dancers" laying track.

Several matters came to the forefront during the summer, including the city council's resolution to ask the mayor to explain why he had not enforced the fender issue. The council also heard more on the delicate matter of race separation; something neither the streetcar companies, railroads, nor the local Jacksonville government wanted to enforce. The state government, however, was determined to push the issue on the city and the railroads. A black member of Jacksonville's City Council, Sixth Ward, stood and explained why the ordinance was completely unnecessary.

News was released that the two streetcar companies had buried the hatchet and would now allow their tracks to cross each other, a vital point for Telfair Stockton's line across the north side. In fact, the citizens were pleased to learn that the new extension was doing a phenomenal business among the residents of the predominantly black section of the city.

In the spring of 1906, the city council heard a proposition for the Jacksonville Electric Company on power distribution. The city charter prohibited competition with the city's power plant operation, and the electric company wanted to extend its lines.

By summer, the council and the street railways were discussing franchises, rules and ordinances and generally fine-tuning the same. By the time the July 20 meeting ended, the city attorney, J.M. Barrs, had the whole affair assigned to a special committee.

The committee met in secret to consider the two bills for the franchises, and members of the respective companies were seen to come and go from the room. The work of fine-tuning the franchises wasn't finished until December 18, but it was perfectly clear that the city would be taking over all of the power distribution business.

The company added an iconic change to the face of Main Street, a change that would become widely known in the tourist trade as the "Most Beautiful Streetcar Line in the World." The board of public works met on June 11 and issued the order for the double tracking of the Main Street Line, starting at the beginning of the parkway segment at Phelps Street and setting the curb lines along the street eighteen inches in toward the property lines on both sides of the street. The result, of course, was a well-built section of track, set slightly above the street grade so the tops of the rails were only an inch or so above street level. The entire line was then sodded over, and lush tropical landscaping was added to each side along with a stately double row of palm trees.

If things were hopping over at the street railways, the South Jacksonville Ferry Company manager C.E. Barr stated that local architecture firm Holmes and McClure had completed plans for the new ferry terminal complete with a 225-foot recreational pier.

Jacksonville seemed to be entering a renewed age of prosperity. By 1908, Mayor W.H. Sebring went to Stone and Webster and the Jacksonville Electric Company and formally requested that the street railway purchase some new streetcars. More specifically, those in the know reported that the cars the mayor had in mind could only be described as "parlor cars." They were in use in many other great urban centers, in Chicago and New York City for example, and it was felt that Jacksonville was once again in the race to the top.

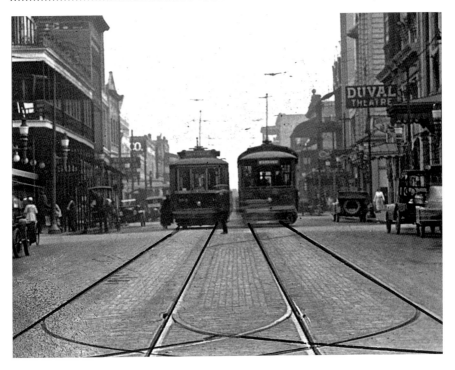

Some long-ago photographer thought it necessary to ink in the track; note the two distinct rooflines. Also, the car on the left has its convertible front windows in, and the other car has its windows removed for the season. *Courtesy of the Jacksonville Historical Society.*

Messrs Stone and Webster
No. 147 Milk Street
Boston, Mass: July: 21, 1908
Gentlemen:
Perhaps in my letter of yesterday I did not make myself quite clear as to what sort of cars we would like to have you place here for the winter, which I think would be largely patronized by the tourists and by our own people.

Two or three regular parlor cars, with portable chairs in them, cane chairs upholstered with leather. In other words, a handsome parlor car, up-to-date, such as you see in Brooklyn, New York, Philadelphia, Chicago, Cleveland, Denver and other large cities.

These cars can be chartered by theater parties and excursionists and private parties, and to be run regular during the tourist season. These cars to be in size fifty-five feet long and in a different color from the regular cars, and to have brass railings on the platform and the inside trimmings to be of blue and maroon color.

These cars would be literally patronized by the tourists with a charge of .25 to .50 cents fare for riding in such cars.

The Local Conditions

We have a summer population here of 60,000 and winter 75,000, so you can readily see that our city warrants such an improvement. "The seeing of Jacksonville," during the winter has become a great fad, and I believe running these cars here would be a profitable investment. We have a very large floating population in winter, and if we could get such cars as are run in the places named in this letter, I am sure they would be well patronized by tourists, councilmen and prominent citizens here and they agree with me that it is their belief that these cars would be liberally patronized.

Awaiting your further reply, I am,

Very Truly

William H. Sebring, Mayor

By August 4, the mayor ramped up his campaign with a article in the *Florida Times-Union* headlined "Mayor Sebring Hot After Those Cars."

By this time, a large number of letters had passed between the city and Stone and Webster. It was also learned that the cars were absolutely headed our way, and the mayor was calling on the citizens to help him push this over the top.

The *Times-Union* quoted the mayor in part about this being the superior means of both entertaining our visitors and having them tour the city

The proof was uttered by the mayor himself:

Touring the City at a nominal cost. Say for instance, by the payment of twenty-five cents they would be afforded the opportunity of sightseeing the City, whereas in the past they have had to pay one dollar to be whirled about the City in a half-satisfactory manner in automobiles.

The tourist [streetcars] cars have many advantages. In the first place there's plenty of room and the appointment is such that usually affords convenience and comfort. Those cars could be chartered, where they here, in the evening by the young people…could be secured and a delightful outing could be spent riding about the City.

I don't think there will be many sight-seeing automobiles operating in the city during the coming winter, as the tax increased for such a business from 50 dollars to 250 dollars a year.

Ortega Traction Company

Excitement became electric all across the city when news was released on July 16, 1904, that Ortega, a new town being developed by former United States senator Wilkinson Call on the St. Johns River's west bank just south of the mouth of McGirts Creek, was to be connected to Jacksonville via a new car line.

The news broke as the steamship *Comanche* of the Clyde Steamship Line docked with a large cargo of streetcar and railroad materials. It was felt that the Jacksonville Electric Company would never extend its lines so far south, so Call and his associates had quietly incorporated the Ortega Traction Company.

Track laying on the long extension south to Ortega had come to a standstill by May 1, 1905, on account of difficulty securing right of way across the Robinson Improvement Company property. As soon as the deeds were transferred to the company, track laying could resume in full force. Senator Call had received assurances that they would buy land at his place.

The county said that they would construct an improved shell road to the property. The Ortega section would eventually have some of the most exclusive property in Florida.

In time, John N.C. Stockton went before the commissioners with a proposal for a new franchise, a street railway and water and electric lines along certain roadways—namely running from the end of St. Johns Avenue to Aberdeen, Aberdeen to Herschel, Herschel to San Juan, San Juan to Grand and Grand to Baltic to the center of Ortega Village. Stockton said the route was laid out for a distance of five miles and that the track was constructed, awaiting approval to erect poles and string wire.

Just thirteen days after the arrival of the track material for the Ortega Traction Company car line, the local papers reported that considerable progress was already being made. The companies had already decided that Jacksonville Electric and Ortega Traction cars would operate as a single line and there would be no change of equipment or transfers.

Suddenly, with the ring of a signal bell and the sound of the familiar trolley gong, Ortega was linked to Jacksonville. It was late October 1908.

Owing to the delay in the arrival of materials, the passing tracks were incomplete. Considering the deplorable city speed restrictions of twelve miles per hour, a single car would run back and forth on an intolerable forty-five-minute headway. Today, the transportation authority is tightening the headways somewhat closer to 1908 levels of a service; in 1908, however, that level of service was considered abhorrent.

John Stockton was an enthusiast of Ortega and the "grand conveyance." Ortega would sport a yacht club, park, village center and country club. With the completion of the Ortega Line, Stockton anticipated the "finest and liveliest city in the south."

Otherwise, in 1908, the streetcars were riding a growth tsunami. Jacksonville's first motion picture studio opened. The first ever Technicolor feature, *The Gulf Between*, was filmed in Jacksonville, as was Oliver Hardy's debut film, *Outwitting Daddy*. Metro Pictures started in Jacksonville and did so well that Marcus Loew bought them out and then purchased Goldwyn Pictures, founded by Samuel Goldfish,[10] to become MGM. It was said that Jacksonville rose like a shooting star, one that unfortunately burned out quickly. More than thirty studios would open in the city as it became the "Winter Film Capital of the World," but by 1930, they were all gone.[11]

Thanks to Mayor Sebring, Jacksonville was informed that the large lounge cars would arrive in December. The people were thrilled at the news; after all, this was like getting a new family car. On arrival, the cars were pressed into immediate service.

By 1909, the streetcars were inadvertently becoming day-care centers and conductors and motormen became trusted family friends. The trick was to put Junior on the trolley, tell the conductors he or she had permission to ride the system, then sit back and relax or tend to errands. Apparently the company didn't mind the revenue, and the streetcar men actually struck up lasting friendships among both the children and families.

On August 10, 1909, the first streetcar climbed up and over the new Adams Street Viaduct. The Seaboard Air Line and St. Johns River Terminal Railroads built the 1,400-foot span in consideration of allowing them to switch freight cars across Bay Street. Just to the north of this, the Duval Street Viaduct had been replaced in 1902, having been largely destroyed in the Great Fire.

The heavy tropical rains of September 10 washed out sections of track and streets throughout the city. In true railroad fashion, the company said they'd be up and running again in a couple of days. The streets didn't fare nearly as well, since many of them were unpaved or surfaced with shell.

By November 1909, the first of the ten new St. Louis built PAYE (Pay As You Enter) streetcars arrived in Jacksonville. The new type of cars was the forerunner of the familiar transit farebox or card validators. No longer would a conductor have to hunt down the new passengers in their seats and collect a fare, burning valuable schedule time. Harvey Croom, manager for the Jacksonville Electric Company stated that all of the company's cars were

Right: Couplers for multiple car operation, the latest in destination curtain signage, gates, PAYE and a polished brass controller set this handsome car apart. *Courtesy of Washington University in St. Louis.*

Below: St. Louis Car Company has rolled car 149 onto the transfer table; it will be moved down the line to receive trucks and finish fittings. *Courtesy of Washington University in St. Louis.*

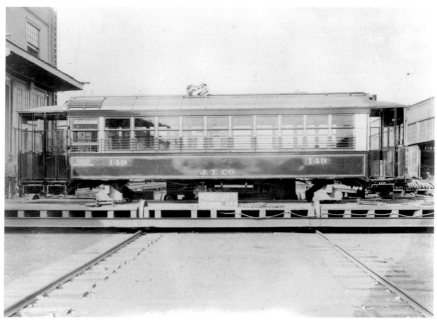

being modified with PAYE meters. This was a sea change in the industry, and though the conductors would remain for a time as glorified doormen, this generally spelled the end of the position. The new cars had folding steps. When the doors opened, steps folded out and down for ease of boarding; close the door, and the steps vanished. This was an important safety device as it eliminated people jumping on and off while the cars were in motion. Another innovation with a rather unique Jacksonville twist were the gated entries in lieu of doors, a nod to our subtropical climate. These entries were extra wide with divided lanes so one line could board while the other line detrained. In case of a rush hour crowd, the passengers could use the rear door to exit. The cars were so cutting edge that this particular feature is just now returning to mass transit in the twenty-first century. The cars had an electric signal bell, whereby passengers could signal the conductor when their stop came up.

Unlike most cars shipped in on railroad flat cars, these were shipped in sections and assembled locally.

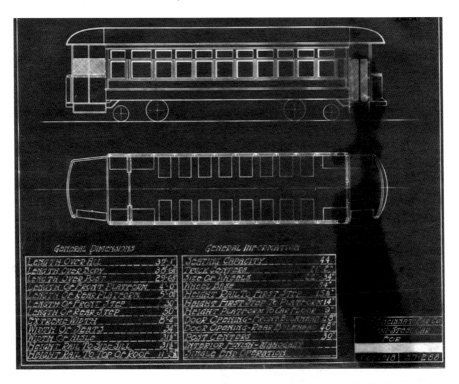

The blueprints for this 1918 order of Cincinnati cars reveals that they were 39.1 feet long overall, seated forty-four passengers and were finished in mahogany. *Courtesy of the Cincinnati Car Company Photographic Collection, Indiana Historical Society.*

The door opening at the rear of the car was a full four feet, and the truck centers were twenty-one feet, two inches. *Courtesy of the Cincinnati Car Company Photographic Collection, Indiana Historical Society.*

The deep cushioned seats were thirty-four inches wide and fully reversible; aisles were thirty-one and a half inches wide. *Courtesy of the Cincinnati Car Company Photographic Collection, Indiana Historical Society.*

These new cars were semiconvertible (the end windshields were removable for air flow) and included the Jacksonville Traction Company's signature gates in lieu of doors; however, the bulkheads had lockable doors. Note the latest in destination signage with a fabric curtain of destination information mounted on rollers that could be easily changed. *Courtesy of the Cincinnati Car Company Photographic Collection, Indiana Historical Society.*

The cars had a mahogany finish, and they were equipped as well as those in America's leading cities. Local Jaxsons were as proud as a muster of peacocks. The new fleet went into service on the Springfield Lines.

The rear entry was truly huge. Note the coupler and lack of a controller at this end; these were rare single-ended cars (single-end operation only) as opposed to the typical double-ended streetcars. They could be coupled back-to-back, forming eighty-eight (seated) passenger trains. *Courtesy of the Cincinnati Car Company Photographic Collection, Indiana Historical Society.*

As the city continued to aggrandize, a new line was laid on Forsyth from Main to Ocean Street and down to Bay—a second downtown loop. The Hogan Street Line was ripped up and new track with seventy-pound rail was laid down. Cars running on the Jacksonville Union Station–Fairfield Line

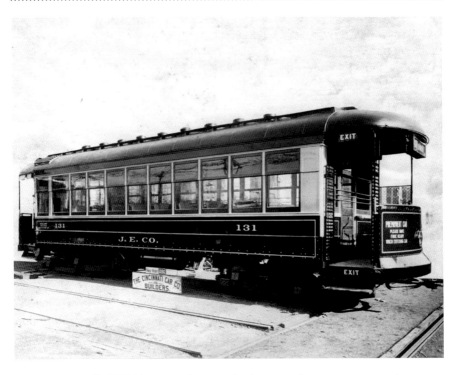

The newest so-called BRT buses are forty-one feet long, seat forty-one persons and are quick to advertise that another twenty to thirty passengers can stand. The new buses also cost well over half a million dollars per vehicle and have a useful life of eight to twelve years. If they keep up the rapid improvements, sometime in the near future, they might actually build a bus as advanced as these streetcars were. Cincinnati built at least two groups of these cars for Jacksonville; the first were delivered prior to 1912, and the next order in 1918. Had we not prematurely junked them, these same streetcars could easily still be in service at the age of one hundred. *Courtesy of the Cincinnati Car Company Photographic Collection, Indiana Historical Society.*

were shifted to the new Adams Street viaduct. By mid-August, the railway had reached fifty route miles.

Finally, Mayor Sebring triumphed in the quest for cars befitting a movie capital and liberally progressive city. By January 1910, the first two long-awaited lounge cars would be on the property. The cars were of the largest type and were convertible for either open or closed operation. They were equipped with oversized seating, colored lighting (typically stained glass) and water fountains and were described as having many others conveniences. The mayor and the company calculated that some twenty to twenty-five miles of beautifully scenic lines were available for tours and charters.

That same year, an extension from Phoenix Park[12] to Cummer's Mill was built—a massive operation along the north-side waterfront that owned its own railroad running from Jacksonville to High Springs. The Jacksonville and Southwestern Railroad was sold to the Atlantic Coast Line Railroad in 1904, but it continued to operate out of the Catherine Street Station; thus, the car line was drawing Cummer business from both the north and south edges of town.

The Great Tram Robbery

On a delightful Sunday evening, September 12, 1910, Jacksonville and Florida experienced their own version of the "Great Train Robbery." The streetcars would slow on the long McGirts Creek Bridge leading to Ortega. Suddenly, three armed men jumped aboard and ordered everyone to put their hands up. The motorman found himself staring down the barrel of a loaded pistol. At the other end of the car, the conductor spotted the commotion and crawled to the front, pulling his own pistol, which then misfired three times. The startled would-be robbers were no doubt focused on the hapless conductor when the other male passengers suddenly attacked them. All three men fled into the night or perhaps over the rail of the bridge and were never seen again. Needless to say, women and children were terrified by the experience. It was never established for certain if they wanted money and valuables or if they were targeting someone on the car itself. Thus Florida's Great Tram Robbery was bravely foiled.

Finally, by October 1910, a large number of people lodged a complaint to the city for not allowing the streetcars to stop at the Bay Street entry of Jacksonville Union Station.

Business was good in June 1910, and the roaring growth of the city and the Jacksonville Electric Company was continuing with the company posting a 22.6 percent increase over the same month a year earlier. Expansion was again on the agenda. There had been a growing chorus of voices for a Pearl Street extension of the streetcar system from North Hogan Street. Presently, the Jacksonville Real Estate Board met with the company officials to entice them to cross Springfield Park and roll up Pearl all the way to the Trout River.

Through the first few months of 1911, a city council special committee held meetings to improve the service on the city's streetcars. Apparently seven-minute headways were intolerable—would that we had such problems today!

A discussion ensued over the steps that folded away on the new cars; the older cars were not so equipped. So the deadly practice of people jumping on the crowded steps of moving cars continued.

In April, one of three electrical accidents recorded during the early years of the Jacksonville Electric Company took place. Two of the generators at the company's electric plant were disabled, dropping the line current and drastically slowing the operation of the cars. The company put an emergency plan in place, and the entire maintenance of the way and electrical force worked through two grueling twenty-four-hour days, with additional manpower from the Merrill-Stevens Shipyard. Finally, regular speeds resumed, and within two days, the crisis was over. Previous incidents included a live wire, which simply snapped, no doubt owing to the technology of the day. A mysterious nighttime incident when something started drawing off line power and slowing the cars. The cause wasn't discovered due to darkness and was quickly fixed in the morning.

JACKSONVILLE TRACTION COMPANY

No sooner had the ink dried on the transfer than a formal permit was issued to the Jacksonville Traction Company (JTCO) to build a new powerhouse across from the carbarns in Brooklyn. The JTCO was investing $500,000 in the new electric plant, which was to have a capability of generating some 3,400 kilowatts, far above the amount needed for the system.

On April 19, 1911, the *Florida Times-Union* announced a historic event: effective on March 31, 1911, the city would take over residential power production, leaving the traction company with very thin operating margins. This may have been survivable, but increasing demands on the company to "share" profit, pave and sweep streets, pay taxes and operate more or less at the whim of City Hall was a recipe for the ultimate failure.

The new company experienced its first accident on May 15, when just before noon, a Main Street Car rear-ended a First and Walnut Car. There were no fatalities, but detective Philip P. Lord was badly battered.

A city council committee for the improvement of the streetcar system met company officials for joint regulation of schedules. Hardy Croom, the Traction Company manager, added that the company wanted to change the way the cars stop. In the future, the JTCO desired to stop all cars on the

NEW COMPANY ABSORBS STREET RAILWAY LINES
JACKSONVILLE ELECTRIC COMPANY
TRANSFERS PROPERTY

A warranty deed was filed yesterday by the Jacksonville Electric Company to the Jacksonville Traction Company for $1 conveying all real estate and personal property including franchises owned by the former company. The Jacksonville Traction Company took over all lands, buildings, generators, dynamos, motors, cars, fixtures, tools and franchises together with all rights of way, benefits and profits accruing conveyed as of March 31, 1911.

The aforesaid property, rights and franchises are subject however to a certain mortgage which has been assumed by the Jacksonville Traction Company as follows: July 14, 1902, Jacksonville Electric Company to the American Trust Company as trustee securing an issue of $1,250,000, face value of said bonds of said Jacksonville Electric Company, bearing date of May 1, 1903.

The transferring of the goods and chattels of the Jacksonville Electric Company to the Jacksonville Traction Company will place the latter company in a position to finance the extensive improvements that are now under course of construction and requiring immediate attention and others which will require attention at a latter date.

The stock of the Jacksonville Electric Company has been exchanged for stock in the Jacksonville Traction Company share for share so that the old stockholders occupy the same position in the new company that they did in the old and the advantage gained by the new company is the ability to raise capital by the means of bonds. Considerable thought and attention was given to this plan, which was carried out, and the interests of the old stockholders have been fairly protected.

The development of the street car business in Jacksonville has been so rapid that it outgrew the capitalization of the Jacksonville Electric Company and it was necessary to provide facilities for financing future improvements with cheap money on an economical basis and in a way free from so-called high finance and with absolute protection to both stock and bondholder of the old company who will fully participate in the new.[13]

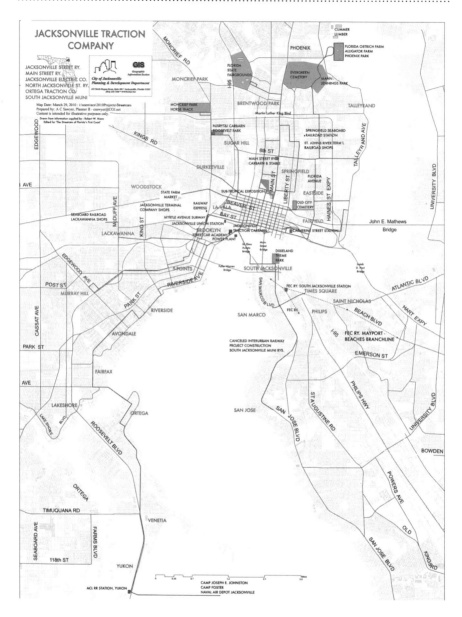

near side of the street. The city accepted the proposal on certain lines for a thirty-day trial.

Another improvement marked the maturity of Jacksonville as a city: express car service. The plan allowed inbound Ortega cars to make their regular stops through Aberdeen Street, running nonstop on St. Johns until they reached downtown. A similar plan was put into action for inbound cars

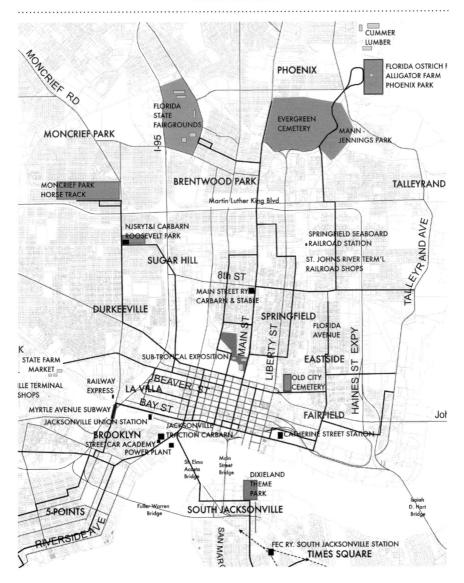

Opposite: Jacksonville Traction map. *Courtesy of the City of Jacksonville GIS mapping.*

Above: Detail of downtown Jacksonville. *Courtesy of the City of Jacksonville GIS mapping.*

from Phoenix Park—regular stops until reaching Main Street and nonstop into downtown. The effort delighted the citizenry; they were thrilled at the idea in practice. The express cars had track superiority over the regular cars and were allowed to overtake them at sidings.

The *Jacksonville Dixie* newspaper ran a shocking headline on May 25, 1912: "The Murdered Streetcar Men." Out on the far east side of the city at the end of the Fairfield Line, conductor T.C. Smith and motorman R.F. Sparkman, beloved employees and family men, were shot without warning by a couple bandits who then ransacked the farebox.

The shocking crime was apparently pulled off by a couple degenerate vagrants. The streetcar men were armed but trained to use restraint. Unfortunately, it appears these men got the jump on them, gunning them down in cold blood.

Apparently there had been some suspicious behavior on the part of certain homeless drifters who had been threatening the car men whenever they were asked to produce a fare or follow the rules. Words such as "I'll get even with you" were bantered about in front of witnesses. A suggestion was made that more latitude would be given to the operators to take immediate action the moment such a threat is uttered.

8
MEN O' WAR

January 1912 was sunny and mild, and the streetcars were omnipresent and overcrowded. Discussions continued in committee about the use of girder rail in place of standard railroad "T rail."[14] The traction company announced it would add special cars to and from Evergreen Cemetery on weekends. Jacksonville Streetcar Academy opened adjacent to the carbarn in Brooklyn and offered courses in railway science. Expansion was rumored throughout the city with great expectations.

Ugliness exploded over the city in the last months of 1912. Flexing its muscle in the height of the Progressive Era, the local Carpenters Union went out on strike in 1902. The Florida Federation of Labor Unions went to the streetcar company and suggested that the employees form a railway union. The Carpenters Union pooled their expertise and resources and helped to fund and promote the new streetcar union. The unionist published a hebdomadal labor newspaper called the *Artisan* that reported the organized labor side of those tumultuous days.

Urban warfare was about to overshadow all of the promise in the air; it appeared that the whole city was starting to fracture along management-labor lines in the last few months of 1912. Former president Theodore Roosevelt said he would be a union member if he was in the labor force, but he blistered both the companies and the unions for unfair labor practices: "Unions are just as much a necessity in our modern industrial nation as a corporation itself. Both must obey the law." Unfortunately, neither side had any intention to be sold a pup.

A proud crew shows off Jacksonville Traction car number 104 on the Florida Avenue Line. The trolley poles on top of the car are spring loaded and the little T-shaped device just above the Florida Avenue destination sign serves as a hook to hold an unused pole down. The "steering wheel" is actually a hand brake, and the long rod hanging to the left of the headlight was inserted into a metal plate in the road to switch tracks, all by leaning out the removable front window. *Courtesy of the Jacksonville Historical Society.*

Long workdays and selling seniority rights were clearly grievances, but the public exposé that one manager was sleeping with the other's wife was shocking. In an attempt to appease the employees and thwart a strike, Stone and Webster immediately fired both gentlemen and instituted a twelve-hour workday. On the downside, the company instituted what it called the "Plan." The Plan was designed for employee intimidation and intelligence gathering. O.J. Drummond, a former detective, was hired as a company spy, but the ruse was short lived as the telegraph messenger boys discovered the truth and blew the whistle. Some of the streetcar men kidnaped Drummond and threatened his life. Reporting his rough handling resulted in several arrests, but his usefulness was spent.

Company executive George Baldwin suggested it was time for the company to take the gloves off, but the company blundered when an employee was discharged for his desire to join a union. Company attorneys said the city was largely sympathetic to the unions, and such action was bound to turn the city against the company.

Worse, the Amalgamated Association of Street and Electric Railway Employees of America, Local 608, stated that the company was making a practice of terminating employees with over three years of service because the third year came with a large pay raise. No reasons were ever given for the practice.

The company fired the initial few who had joined the union and then, for the coup de grâce, fired virtually everyone who had joined the union, resulting in a walkout.

Since October 18, 1912, there had been a growing feeling of unrest within the traction company. For ten days, the company had been closely monitoring the activities of the employees until, on the twenty-eighth, the majority of the employees refused to report for work. The few who did report to work explained that they were afraid to take cars out on the line because of threats made against them. As a result, only five of the normal fifty-two cars actually went out onto the streets, and these were withdrawn by nightfall.

A former streetcar conductor from New York named James "Boss" Farley formed a company of strikebreakers. Farley would sell the services of his New York toughs to any company on strike. When Stone and Webster hired Farley's army of scabs, the reaction was immediate. The city exploded as other unions joined in the melee. The striking streetcar men attacked the Jacksonville Board of Trade, as they were responsible for hiring the police commissioner.

Jacksonville was paralyzed; the streetcar company was in for the fight of its life. Management imported strikebreakers from northern cities, and by

A victim of unknown vandals and dating from the "Great Streetcar Strike," car 137 rides the transfer table to the repair shop. *Courtesy of Washington University in St. Louis.*

CHAPTER 999, OFFENCES AGAINST THE PUBLIC PEACE, ARTICLE 1, AFFRAYS, RIOTS, ROUTS AND UNLAWFUL ASSEMBLIES, SECTION 3243, "WHEN KILLING IS EXCUSED"

If, by reason of the efforts made by any of said officers or by their direction to disperse such assembly, or to seize and secure the persons composing the same, who have refused to disperse, any such person or other person present is killed or wounded, the said officers and all persons acting by their order or under their direction shall be held guiltless.[15]

the thirtieth, the cars were operating again. Rioting broke out. It was bad enough that they brought in strikebreakers; it was unthinkable that they brought in Yankees, and the old sectional rivalries thundered onto the streets. The company had seriously miscalculated southern sympathies; the badly beaten Yankees returned to the barn. Operations would be determined at a conference between company, civil and military authorities.

Mayor Jordan laid down the law in a proclamation that forbade residents from public assemblies and vocal exhibitions referencing the Florida Statutes.

In a meeting with the mayor and city council, a resolution was drafted requesting that troops not be sent to Jacksonville for fear of expanding the battlefront. A meeting between Mayor Jordan, Sheriff Bowden, Police Chief Vinzant, Chairman Bostwick of the board of bond trustees and members of the police committee immediately reversed that notion. The police department said they were incapable of preserving order. Bostwick didn't support the union, and when Sheriff Bowden said the police force was made up almost exclusively of fired three-year streetcar employees, fear rippled through the meeting. A sympathetic judge who supported unionization undermined the sheriff's first arrests. He accused the sheriff's department and the traction company as being one and the same. Governor Gilchrist ordered Major General J.C.R. Foster to Jacksonville with the necessary troops.

Battalions of khaki-clad soldiers swarmed over the streetcars and streets; it was a surreal quiet.

Citizens' committees, delegations of current and former traction company employees, the military, the police, the city and every other combination of power were holding endless meetings to resolve the crisis. In spite of the best intentions, by the early morning hours of November 4, it appeared hopeless.

Three striking car men were arrested for throwing brickbats at the trolley cars. An arrest was also made for the attempted assault on the life of police lieutenant Fred Roach, as well as the trashing of five trolleys during the day and making bodily injury threats to passengers, including local ladies. The state troops had a handful when the first cars ventured onto the LaVilla Line. Several hundred strike sympathizers had gathered in Monroe Street just east of Davis, and as cars approached, it was apparent that this was about to escalate. As one car tried to pass, the mobs attacked; the wise motorman threw on full power and quickly sped; the speeding streetcar, however, was badly damaged by flying missiles.

The position of the two sides was inexorable; the Jacksonville Traction Company management was adamant that it would never recognize the Amalgamated Association of Street and Electric Railway Employees of America, and the streetcar employees were equally unyielding that they be recognized.

Daily arrests continued to be made for throwing missiles and smashing windows. Other striking employees were determined to become more creatively lethal, and they began to employ motorcycles and automobiles in their attempts to catch and board the cars and assault the operators. It was becoming obvious that even more militant steps would be needed to suppress the strike as a car on the corner of Main and Beaver Street was fired into, the bullet narrowly missing two passengers. Finally, car number 110 was attacked from an ambush between the Ortega River Bridge and Riverside, causing a number of passengers to be injured by flying bricks and glass.

Colonel Cromwell Gibbons opened his own jail in a city street and told the *Florida Times-Union*, "We could end the strike today if we had sufficient bullets for our weapons." This inflammatory statement resulted in the colonel being immediately relieved of command. If the importation of northerners set off a bomb, it was also instrumental in soothing local resentments. No longer was the company, the union, the white or black employee or manager the problem: all sides blamed the outsider "foreigners" and "Yankees." George Baldwin, the manager of the company, said, "We could end the strike, but we'd have to recognize the black workers equal to white workers." And though all unions had joined together to have a general strike, it was the black unionists who made impassioned speeches for no strike. With the black unions serving as peacemakers, (no doubt fearful of retaliation) the general strike threat went away.

Things began to settle down as the reality of paying the rent and feeding the families became the better part of valor. On November 10, Governor Gilchrist ordered a schedule of troop withdrawals with the civil authorities of the City of Jacksonville stepping into the void. On the fourteenth, the traction company cars of the Springfield Line were recalled about noon to the carbarn in Riverside, where a group of employees who had participated in strike awaited reinstatement. Within a few moments, those cars were headed back north toward Springfield with their regular operators once again at the controls. Eighty-four of the remaining strikers assembled in the Hall of the Central Trades And Labor Council at the corner of Bay and Liberty Streets and voted fifty-eight to twenty-six to renounce the union and apply for their old jobs back.

The three-week strike was finally over, but it'd been terribly costly to the company. Investigations discovered union sympathetic employers had fired many of the National Guard soldiers from their full-time jobs. Realizing that the strike itself had so taxed the ability of the state to respond to the emergency, Governor Gilchrist applied for a loan in the amount of $15,379.05 from the City of Jacksonville to make up for the shortfall of funds in the state military budget.

Now that peace had finally descended on Jacksonville, the city and its traction company again demonstrated amazing resilience. By mid-December, the company sought and got permission to use just one of its tracks on the Broad Street Viaduct as it vigorously replaced the second track. Elsewhere, there was consideration for extending the Florida Avenue Line out Howard Street and for pushing the Main Street Line toward Panama Park.

9
ON THE LOOSE

As the calendar turned another page, the local newspapers were running large photo spreads of the new power station (located where the *Times-Union* building is today) and the newly expanded and improved carbarn. The city council granted the traction company's request for twelve months to complete the new Hogan–Pearl Street and Newnan–Walnut Street Lines.

In early 1913, permission was granted by public works to start on the Lemon Street Line (today's College Street, though the line was actually built one block farther west on Banana Street, today's Dellwood Avenue). This was the start of the Murray Hill Line. The construction of this new extension introduced another innovation to the street railway system as the local newspapers snapped photos of the use of "electric welders."

Concurrent with the new route, ten new "Turtleback" cars arrived from the St. Louis Car Company. These cars featured air-powered doors and steps, as well as comfortable seating for forty-four passengers. An ingenious ventilation system kept the cars as open as possible, while at the same time eliminating areas that would gather dust and dirt, making these cars quite sanitary. They were placed into service as soon as they arrived, allowing the company to pull some of the older cars out of the regular lineup to be used as reserve coaches when the need arose.

The company was enjoying the fruits of its lushly landscaped car routes, which were gaining world renown. The city handed down a decision on November 20 stating that the company should also maintain those green parkways. When the McGirts Creek Bridge experienced some trouble, the

Jacksonville Traction operated a large fleet of the "bouncing babies" single-truck Birneys. Murray Hill, Ortega and Brentwood were among its many regular assignments. A troublesome prank was encountered when the boys at Lee High School discovered that packing one end platform of the car could derail it. *Courtesy of Washington University in St. Louis.*

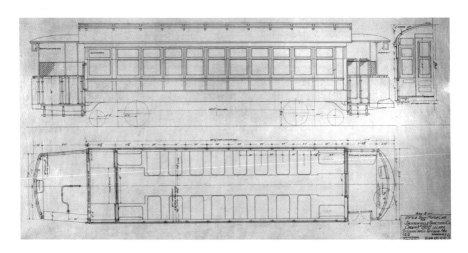

The St. Louis Car Company was a favored supplier, as this drawing of its August 31, 1911 version of our Turtleback car testifies. *Courtesy of Washington University in St. Louis.*

Another Turtleback is born at the St. Louis Car Company plant, a great example of expert fitting. *Courtesy of Washington University in St. Louis.*

county commissioners ordered the company to repair the bridge and reopen the Ortega Line within forty-eight hours.

Archduke Franz Ferdinand of Austria and his wife, Sophie, Duchess of Hohenberg, were shot dead in Sarajevo by Gavrilo Princip on June 28, 1914. The murder of the heir presumptive to the Austro-Hungarian

Left: A view of the bulkheads and doors behind the operator. Note the exotic wood, incredible workmanship, polish and brass fittings. Modern rubber-tired faux "trolleys" built on cab and chassis (the type used for delivery trucks) are not even close in quality. But the faux fleet has given birth to a new moniker locally, a play on the old PCC (Presidents Conference Car) Streetcars; they're known locally as PCTs (Potato Chip Trucks). *Courtesy of Washington University in St. Louis.*

Below: There are no plywood or hard-slatted wooden seats aboard this new car. *Courtesy of Washington University in St. Louis.*

Brand-new car 137, sitting on unique shop trucks, shows off its equally unique and trend-setting gates (as opposed to doors) designed for both traffic and air flow. These cars were the subject of national industry attention. *Courtesy of Washington University in St. Louis.*

throne set in motion a horrific domino effect that launched the world into World War I.

By the end of the year, with America staying neutral and out of the fight, Murray Hill suffered a delay in being brought into the Jacksonville Traction System. This line followed Edison Avenue to Dellwood, to Margaret Street, to Myra Street, to Stockton Street and to College Street southwest, crossing the Atlantic Coast Line Railroad at grade on College Street. It then continued running southward through the green parkway between the railroad tracks and Plymouth Street, to Nelson Street, to Corby Street and to Edgewood Avenue in Edgewood Village. Adding a return leg from Edgewood Avenue to Plymouth Street completed the loop.

The traction company launched its first safety campaign in May 1915. B.T. Longino, a safety expert, stated records for the end of the month of May showed a 50 percent decrease in incidents. This was significant as the years 1913–15 were heavily involved in injury claims and litigation.

The oft-talked-about girder rail made its appearance in 1916, and then a major sewerage, water and gas main overhaul was conducted by the city downtown. Just prior to repaving, the company re-laid girder rail on Forsyth Street between Main and Laura. By December, the traction company had laid double track across Springfield Park to Cedar Street and on into Hogan, completing the Hogan–Pearl Street Line.

On April 6, 1917, the United States formally declared war against Germany and entered World War I. The city and the traction company shifted to a wartime footing. On July 18, at the request of W.T. Edwards, the public service committee of the city council instructed the company to run more cars on the Phoenix Line, and on the thirtieth, new car service started running from Eighth and Fisher Streets to the Talleyrand industrial and port area.

The army readied construction of its huge training base at the state campground on Black Point on the west bank of the St. Johns River. Camp Johnston was named for General Joseph E. Johnston (February 3, 1807– March 21, 1891).

While it was a most welcome neighbor, the new camp placed a heavy demand on the primitive roadway between the post and the city. Major Frederick Wheeler, constructing quartermaster of the new camp, and members of his staff arrived on September 26, 1917. He revealed that plans called for a camp that would house some fifteen thousand men immediately, continuing with construction to reach a twenty-five-thousand-man capacity. Even this came with provision for quick enlargement of the whole quartermaster camp to an ultimate forty thousand men within a few months.

Finally, on Christmas Day 1917, the long-awaited plan was announced: "Line Will Be a Fine Xmas Gift to Soldiers in Camp." The Duval County Commission approved the project on Christmas Eve. The traction company had been meeting with the commission for several weeks but wouldn't utter a "chirp in a carload" about any possible expansion.

When the moment finally came, Stone and Webster's powerful Boston attorney, Mayland H. Morse Esquire, placed his name front and center on the petition. The document itself was written in typical legalese, but it offers us a wonderful window into the past and the details of this very rural car line.

Ultimately the city published, "Resolved, That the Public Service Committee, while it has no jurisdiction over the street railway company, outside of the city limits, wishes to go on record as approving the movement of our citizens to have the street car line extended to Black Point, and will use all its influence with the street car company towards getting same built."

The long awaited petition was finally forthcoming:

"Be it resolved, That the petition of Mayland H. Morse requesting authorization and approval of this board for the location, construction, operation and maintenance by the said Mayland H. Morse, his heirs or assigns, of a line of electric street railway along certain of the highways of Duval County, to-wit:

From present end of car line of the Jacksonville Traction Company on Seminole Avenue in Ortega along Seminole Avenue to Ortega Boulevard to Arapahoe Avenue; thence along Arapahoe Avenue to the south side of Fifth Street, all the above streets and boulevards being in Ortega tract, as recorded in plat book 3, page 10, of the public records of Duval County, Florida.

Also commencing on what is now known as New York Avenue, as shown on the attached plat, at the north side of what is now known as One Hundred and Fourth Street, in the said County of Duval and State of Florida, thence southerly along said New York Avenue to a point where New Road from Yukon Station to State Camp grounds intersects said New York Avenue, a distance of 1.07 miles, more or less be and the same is hereby granted.

And the said Mayland H. Morse, his heirs or assigns, is hereby empowered and given the exclusive rights to lay, maintain and use such tracks, switches and sidings and to place, erect, maintain and use such poles, wires and fixtures over, across and upon the said public highways as may be necessary and proper for the construction, operation and maintenance of an electric street railroad, and to cut down or trim any and all trees along the said public highways as shall be necessary to keep his wires clear by at least one foot, and also to put in place all necessary guy wires and brace poles, and to attach guy wires to trees along said public highways."

On Monday, April 15, 1918, at 5:04 a.m., the streetcars started rolling between Main and Bay Streets downtown and Camp Johnston. The big double-truck streetcars prominently displayed their new destination curtains announcing CAMP JOHNSTON on each end of the car. Due to wartime conditions, the equipment for the 104th Street electrical substation hadn't arrived yet. The traction company had planned to purchase power from the city and feed it into their wires at that point, but because of the delay, they had to start with a reduced service. The fare on the new line was set at a flat fifteen cents, and transfers were accepted to and from all other routes with an additional ten-cent fare. Streetcars to Camp Johnston would follow the operational plan set up for the long run to Ortega and would operate nonstop from downtown to the camp. Just as soon as the new substation got up and running, the cars shifted to ten-minute "double-headed service," running in two car trains, equivalent in capacity to five-minute headways, a level of service virtually unimaginable today.

Concurrent with the opening of the Camp Johnston car line, a tradition started in Jacksonville, which quickly spread across the country. Promptly at 6:00 p.m., as the flags all around the city were lowered, the conductors ordered the cars to stop and announced, "Would you please remove your hats and stand to the colors as our flags are lowered." Perhaps originating with the employees, the first time they did this, the engines at the powerhouse nearly accelerated to their own ruin, but not wanting to kill a great patriotic idea, the company then set staggered times for each line, and from that time on, within minutes of that hour, the cars would stop and the tradition was established.

The following excerpts offer a rare glimpse into the streetcar era in Jacksonville:

• •

SERVING SOLDIERS AND SHIPYARDS AT JACKSONVILLE COMPANY HAS BUILT 3-MILE EXTENSION TO CAMP JOHNSTON AND MAY ADD 1½ MILES—MAN SHORTAGE IS A PROBLEM

These are distinctly marked as giving through express service to Camp Johnston for a 15¢ fare. The condition is a peculiar one, because up to the end of the old Ortega Line, the fare is only 5¢. The restriction is necessary, however, to separate effectively the local rider from the through passenger.

. . . .

FACILITIES FOR TEN-MINUTE SERVICE

Although the extension is single track for unit-car operation, every curve is double tracked and there are six passing tracks within the 3-mile distance. If necessary, therefore, a ten-minute service could be given. At present a thirty-minute service is run between 5 a.m. and 12 o'clock midnight, except for four outbound cars to camp are added between 5 a.m. and 6 a.m. and four inbound cars between 5 p.m. and 6 p.m. To avoid dead mileage these four cars stay at the camp all day while the crews are at work elsewhere or on leave.

. . . .

TRYING TO MEET THE MAN SHORTAGE

Like so many other electric railways, the Jacksonville Traction Company finds it hard to compete with the tremendous wages paid by the shipyards and other war industries. Matters actually reached the point where the employment agent of the shipbuilders promised to take no more railway men, for he realized that this would simply hurt shipbuilding interests more than it would aid them. Since America's participation in the war, the company has raised wages three times. The company saves large sums of money for its men by selling groceries to them at cost. The business amounts to $8,000 a month for 350 men. This policy is carried to the point of competing with the credit grocer, for if the railway man lacks the cash he can get a $5 coupon book, provided he has an equivalent amount of cash coming to him.

The salesroom adjoins the carhouse. It has no running charges of importance except $50 a month for the boy in charge. The service originally included delivery, but this was found too costly. All business is now done over the counter, either with the men themselves or with their families.

Because of the shortage of men, however, the company recently published an advertisement for four weeks in seven county papers. This has brought in country boys, some of whom are only seventeen years of age. In fact war conditions have also forced the company to engage men over fifty years of age. It is not improbable that women will be tried this autumn. If so, they will be put on lines in high-grade residential districts.

In all from 6000 to 8000 men are employed in shipbuilding at present, although the Marine Railway and Drydock Company alone expects to employ 5000 men eventually. Its site, if thus built up, would call for a ¾-mile extension. Housing has not yet presented any problem. One reason is that from 5000 to 6000 negro laborers were taken out of Jacksonville last year.

• •

As the result of war activities the population of Jacksonville, Fla., and vicinity has increased from 80,000 to 100,000 or more. This has not made it necessary, however, for the Jacksonville Traction Company to purchase new cars, for the business to-day has simply gone back to where it was before the depression of 1914. Except in the case of Camp Joseph E. Johnston, the company has not needed to build new track and give special service.

• •

$160,000 TO PROVIDE TRANSPORTATION FOR 20,000 AT THE GREAT QUARTERMASTERS CAMP

The big problem of the company to date has been to take care of Camp Joseph E. Johnston, the great quartermasters' camp of the country where thousands of men are trained for work from shoeing horses to writing shorthand. This camp is 10 miles from the heart of Jacksonville. Its personnel run as high as 20,000. As in the case of other cantonments, the travel is spasmodic and variable in amount. The nearest line, which the company had for serving the camp, was the Ortega Line. This was extended 3 miles and opened for service on April 15. To do this, any rail that came to hand had to be used, from 56 lb. T to 122 lb. girder. The latter, of course, will be replaced with T rail and used in the city when times have changed for the better.

Even with this extension the railway does not go through the camp. It merely reaches the entrance at which point government-controlled autobuses carry people through the grounds. The fare on the streetcar is 15ᶜ; on the buses 10ᶜ, the government is now urging the company to extend its line another 1-½ miles in order to serve the entire camp for the same 15ᶜ fare.

The camp has no prepayment area, but from 4 p.m. to 7 p.m. a man is stationed at the terminal to sell tickets in advance at 15ᶜ straight. In this way the loading is greatly facilitated, as making change for a 15ᶜ fare is painfully slow. To assist the company in the safe and orderly loading of cars, the government also furnishes a platform guard who is relieved by a second soldier about 3:30 p.m.

Owing to the low voltage, the 10-mile trip now requires an hour instead of forty-five minutes. Soon there will be in operation, however, a 500-kw, Westinghouse motor-generator placed in a corrugated shed 1 mile from the terminal. This will raise the voltage sufficiently to permit the run to be made in forty-five minutes, or in one hour if the 1-½ mile extension through the camp is built. The total cost of the substation and of the 3-mile extension already built will be about $160,000.

While the company has not had to buy any cars, it is changing some open cars for one-way operation by the simple expedient of cutting off one running board and screening the side so that it will be impossible for passengers to jump off.

. . . .

MUCH SHIPBUILDING UNDER WAY

Most of the shipyard work at Jacksonville is on the opposite shore of the St. Johns River. The employees from the yards go via ferry to Jacksonville, where they board cars for various lines. The largest single shipbuilding enterprise is that of the Merrill-Stevens Company, which has six 6000-ton and four 10,000-ton steel vessels on the ways. Another of the 5 Jacksonville plants has 12 ways for wooden ships and is building three 5000-ton vessels. Still another plant is building submarine chasers.

• •

Another major event in the city and its street railway history happened on July 10, 1917, when the voters of Duval County passed a bill to issue bonds for the construction of a bridge across the St. Johns River in downtown Jacksonville. The project had been long talked about, taking twenty-five years to get before the voters, and it certainly had its share of antagonists, a situation that was ultimately solved in court. The bonds were issued and sold on July 22, 1919, and contracts were awarded the Missouri Valley Bridge and Iron Company and the Bethlehem Steel Bridge and Iron Company. Finally, on July 1, 1921, Miss Katherine Wilson christened the new span the "Jacksonville–St. Johns River Bridge." The bridge would ultimately become known as the St. Elmo Acosta Bridge, as Acosta championed this and many other civic improvements. Remember, too, that Acosta was connected with a proposed interurban railway to the beaches, and perhaps as a result, the bridge included double tracks even though there was no car line on the south side of the river when it opened. The bridge intersected the Bridge Street Viaduct (what would later become the Riverside Viaduct on the Jacksonville side of the river, the newer viaduct over the railroad yards having replaced an earlier wooden one in 1905).[16]

The same election in 1917 saw conservative Democrat John W. Martin elected mayor; he was determined to "clean up" the movie industry and successfully destroyed it—the third huge economic disaster had befallen Jacksonville.

Shortly after the Camp Johnston Line opened, the traction company's employees again went out on a short-lived strike. The traction company had granted its employees a two-cents-per-hour pay increase, but the employees were determined to win more as well as recognition of their union. After a mass meeting at the Duval Theater, where several prominent people addressed the men, the employees decided to walk out. By June 13, the company offered employees a 12 percent wage increase and reinstatement of certain employees who had been dismissed but not the official recognition of the union. Nevertheless, the executive committee accepted the company's settlement and service cranked up again within the week. Public sentiment was definitely against the traction company employees in this short strike due to the "outrage" of walking out during a war.

10
NOTHING BUT TROUBLE

A far greater enemy than Yellow Jack, the "Spanish Lady" came calling in late 1918, and the city suffered a fourth economic setback. This worldwide influenza pandemic known as the Spanish Lady would ultimately kill more than 50 million people.[17] By October 3, 1918, the company was forced to hire its first group of female conductors. The manpower shortage was acute from the war effort, and the new plague was decimating the ranks of world cities, especially those with a large military contingent. By October, only half of the regular streetcar fleet was actually out on the streets, due to the raging epidemic.

Jacksonville instituted a self-imposed quarantine, but with some effort, it could be circumvented. Those circumventing the lines didn't manage to escape the dread disease; they did, in any case, guarantee that the rest of the state would suffer just as much.

The war ended with Germany's surrender at 11:00 a.m. on November 11, 1918, but by this time, the world was undergoing devastation worse than the black plague of the Middle Ages.

The traction company had just expanded with a long extension through a rural area to the camp, and it quickly became clear that the army had no intention of staying. The employees got a 12 percent increase in wages, and serviceable cars were now at only 50 percent. Add to this profit sharing to the city; state, county and city taxes; paving assessments; and a tenacious refusal by the city to consider a fare increase. Allowed to simmer, these issues would rise and fall from the public eye, but their combined weight would soon enough serve to paint a huge target on Jacksonville's beloved traction company. Though the blowout wouldn't materialize for another eight years, one could truthfully say the handwriting was on the wall.

At the close of the Great War, the company operated 57.73 miles of track and 118 cars.

With financial desperation setting in, on January 8, 1919, the company petitioned the city council to call an election (at their own expense, as was required by the various charters) to raise the fares. To better ascertain the company's position, the city council committee chose to employ an accounting firm to do a full audit of the company's books. The report revealed that for the first time since the days of the Main Street Railway and North Jacksonville Street Railway Town and Improvement Company, the expenses exceeded receipts by some $50,000 dollars. If the Jacksonville Traction Company didn't get some relief and get it soon, disaster loomed.

By August, the city council tossed out the report, and with little relief in sight, Councilman Barrs went after the value of the property and asked for an exact date for the proposed fare increase. Then along came Mayor John W. Martin, who vetoed the whole unpopular effort. Predictably, on October 31, the United States District Court appointed E.J. Triay receiver for the Jacksonville Traction Company. True to a growing Jacksonville form, no sooner had Triay settled into his new job than the city attorney, P.H. Odom, petitioned to intervene and stop the appointment.

As in nature, the moment the company appeared sick or injured, the predators began to pile on. As 1921 dawned, the State Railroad Commission issued an order denying the petition to increase fares. Next, a federal court ordered that the traction company was required to pave Bay Street between its tracks. Once again, the traction company presented evidence of its suddenly shaky financial condition. This time, volumes of more-detailed reports, filed by Triay in November, finally got the attention of the State Railroad Commission. A federal court judge granted permission to E.J. Triay for the Jacksonville Traction Company to issue certificates of indebtedness for $65,000.

On December 2, the federal receiver was able to push through a measure in the Florida Supreme Court to approve a petition for increased fares before the railroad commission. Effective December 15, 1920, the new fares were a whopping increase from five cents to seven cents. They allowed for school fares ten tickets for forty cents, while the Camp Johnston Line was set at a respectable twenty-one cents, up from fifteen cents.

In 1922, control of the company went fully to the creditors, and Stone and Webster sent in John P. Ingle, receiver, as the new manager. Ingle arranged for the creditors to accept new notes for the principal and interest, which amounted to $1,369,000. He also said that Atlantic, Barnett and the local National Bank would be repaid, along with any local judgments, but the out-of-town creditors would have to get in line. Ingle's ability to get along with almost anyone and become a friend to the city, the media and the public would buy the company another ten years and the system another fourteen.[18]

It was John Ingle who laid out a "streetcar manifesto," which starts out historically correct then becomes a truism as spot on as anything ever said about fixed-rail transit.

The future of the Jacksonville Traction Company is a problem, which still must be solved. No community can prosper without an adequate transportation system, and in a city as large as this, streetcars are essential. The company has given excellent service in the past, is now in splendid physical condition and needs only to be put in a position where it can attract new capital in order to continue to provide the additional service for this rapid growth.

Early in the year, the City of South Jacksonville inaugurated a new bus service between Hemming Park downtown and Fletcher Park in South Jacksonville.

Finally, the city council amended Section 5 of the street railway ordinances that required both a motorman and conductor on every car. While it would seem on the surface that half of the car men in the city would be out of work, the company merely reassigned the former conductors to other cars, thus increasing service. In a huge cost-cutting measure, the traction company ordered twenty brand-new one-man Birney Safety Cars, which needed no conductor position. Meanwhile, elsewhere in Florida, Miami cut the fares on the causeway to Miami Beach to five cents and the St. Petersburg Municipal Railways reported its business was up over 30 percent.

In 1920, almost any city in the country with a population over about 10,000 had its own streetcar system, and with very few exceptions, they were privately owned. Former United States Senate antitrust attorney Bradford Snell has estimated that during the early twenties, only one in ten citizens owned an automobile, 90 percent of all trips were made by rail across some 1,200 unique streetcar and electric interurban railroad systems, operating some 44,000 miles (71,000 km) of track, with 300,000 employees, 15 billion annual riders and $1 billion in income. Indeed, in the early part of the century, one in every eleven heads of households worked for the railroad or electric railways.

In the midst of what might seem like doom and gloom to the modern reader, Florida started rising on a spectacular real estate tsunami known as the "Great Florida Boom" of the 1920s. Florida started seeing a huge influx of new residents, and real estate speculators invaded the state in force. As the bubble began to inflate, millions of dollars were being spent on development, and entire new cities were being laid out, parceled and sold off, usually to northern investors. Florida was being sold as a healthy and endless summer paradise. A huge illuminated billboard went up in New York City during the winter months proclaiming, "It's June in Miami." Jacksonville certainly wasn't immune to the effects of the explosion of new residents. The newly opened Union Station of the Jacksonville Terminal Company was forced to expand to thirty-two tracks. Jacksonville Terminal's traffic soared as the gateway to Florida and the point where all railroad routes diverged. For a short time during the peak of the boom, Jacksonville Union Terminal was the busiest station in the world.

Entire cities rose from the pine forests and sawgrass, including Naples, Hollywood and Coral Gables, developed by George Merrick (a proponent of street railways), just to name a few. The established cities like Jacksonville and their businesses invested heavily in new infrastructure to support this "American Rivera." Certainly the cash-strapped Jacksonville Traction Company was no different.

The second bus inroad also came out of the small city of South Jacksonville; the city council passed an ordinance allowing the city to purchase and operate a bus line valued at $40,000. On April 5, transportation advocates for the new municipal operation in the city held a rally for the purpose of brainstorming the proposal.

This bus effort predated the "Streetcar Conspiracy" orchestrated by General Motors president Alfred P. Sloan, who charged his "special unit" formed in 1922 to buy up and scrap the private streetcar systems, convert them to buses and then dump the buses on the cities. The tactic became known as "bustitution," meaning to "busify," or to scrap rail in favor of buses, which GM happily provided—for a price. Once this brilliant cartel made up principally by General Motors, Standard Oil, Phillips 66, Firestone, Mack Trucks (a bus manufacturer) and the Federal Engineering Corporation got rolling, there was no end to dirty tricks and outrageous, unethical conduct. These unscrupulous practices continued right through the 1940s. In Tampa, for example, to sway the vote and "convince" the city councilmen of the superiority of the supposedly flexible buses[19] and for their votes to scrap the rail system, every councilman received the gift of a new LaSalle (Cadillac). In Minneapolis, the local managers scrapped a fleet of brand-new streetcars and then pocketed the proceeds from salvaged metals.

The new plunderbund would visit a target city and make large deposits in the local banks; thus established, they opined that the banks should not extend any new credit to street railways.

Things again picked up for the Jacksonville Traction Company during the banner year of 1923, at least everything except the finances, though the company did institute streetcar advertising. On March 3, new one-man cars started circling into Springfield and, on April 16, into Brentwood. During the year, work was also started on the Hogan Street Line.

The county commission met to consider Commissioner Acosta's plan for an interurban line to the beaches. Acosta was pushing for a popular vote on a trolley line to the beach. You will recall that Acosta served as the secretary of the Jacksonville and Seashore Electric Association, formed in 1917 to continue the dream of connecting the city with the beaches, and he certainly hadn't given up hope. Acosta more than likely foresaw the soon demise of the Florida East Coast Railroad's line from South Jacksonville to Mayport via Saint Nicholas, Spring Glen, Hogan, Hodges, San Pablo, Jacksonville Beach, Neptune Beach and Atlantic Beach, complete with a branchline running from Jacksonville Beach to what would become Ponte Vedra Beach. This was a subject of newspaper headlines that warned, "Time May Kill Beach Trains." Application had been made to the Interstate Commerce Commission to discontinue service. However, Acosta's group was certain the interurban could prevail where the steam road faltered.

After all of the hoopla over municipal ownership of the streetcar lines, one would expect that Acosta's beach interurban would have sailed right through the city commission. Such was not to be as St. Elmo's Trolley crashed into the "sound judgment" of the commission. On April 5, the full commission deferred action on the line to the beach, as in its judgment, it felt the resolution would place it on record as saying the City of Jacksonville should build, equip, own and operate a railway from downtown, across the river and all the way to the beach. The city attorney Odom advised against the resolution, telling the commissioners that he had studied this for over four years and still couldn't recommend it. Acosta countered that the interurban would not bankrupt the city but make it rich.

During the meeting, Chairman W.A. Evans told the commissioners that if "the plan to consolidate the city with the County of Duval moved forward, the city could then require the Jacksonville Traction Company to build the new railway." Acosta offered that if the traction company was still in the hands of a receiver, it could not be made to do anything. Commissioners Frank H. Owen and Thomas C. Imeson both rejected the wording in the proposal, Owen feeling it would bankrupt the city, and Imeson objected to the idea of the city operating mass transit.

Acosta suggested that if they would just put this to a vote, it would carry with a five-to-one margin. Behind the "sticky plaster" of prosperity, a more ominous storm was on the horizon. In only eight years, Japan would invade Manchuria, and the good commissioner must have felt a bit like Emperor Meiji the Great when he wrote:

> *The seas of the four directions—all are born of one womb:*
> *Why, then, do the wind and waves rise in discord?*

Finally the vote came up on April 11, 1923. At 3:00 p.m., the city commission adopted a modified draft of Acosta's resolution. This time around with revised and noncommittal wording, only commissioner Doctor M.B. Herlong and commissioner Owen still opposed it.

"Whereas a great many citizens of the City of Jacksonville feel that an electric car line should be operated over the bridge and to the Atlantic Ocean; and

"Whereas some of these citizens feel that it would be advisable to at this time secure legislative authority for a bond issue for this purpose, or an act which would authorize the City of Jacksonville to construct and operate the line out of the profits from the electric light plant; and

"Whereas the City Commission does not at this time care to record itself as being either in favor of or opposed to the proposition, but has no objection to the matter being submitted to the voters;

"Now therefore, be it resolved, that the City Attorney be and he is hereby directed to prepare and submit to Duval County's legislative representatives such an act for passage at the present session of the legislature as well enable the proposition to be submitted to and passed upon by the city's qualified electors."

Chairman Evans agreed wholeheartedly with Acosta that the board should either endorse it or reject it. Imeson didn't support the plan, but he did believe it should go before the voters. Things were still coming undone; the efforts to amend the resolution and get it to Tallahassee to push the legislature for adoption failed and Acosta said he would do it himself, as he was confident he could succeed. Unfortunately, the project was shelved again.

11

ONE GOOD TURN

About the first of May, Stone and Webster joined a study for the streetcar routes planned in the City of South Jacksonville. E.J. Triay, receiver of the JTCO, handed a proposed contract for the operation of the South Jacksonville car line to Federal Judge R.W. Call. And once again, the railway interests and the local government clashed. The Duval County Board met for the purpose of charging a toll to any streetcar of the South Jacksonville line passing over the new drawbridge across the St. Johns River. Naturally, the meeting exploded into heated arguments and accusations. The City of South Jacksonville stated that the board was hostile to its interests and made statements against the smaller sister city, accusations Dr. Carswell vehemently denied.

Meanwhile, about the time a number of new betterments were on the way, a delegation of citizens met in the city to request the traction company to expand the Brentwood Car Line out beyond the terminus. Mr. Ingle announced better service was coming to Avondale with the addition of six new, one-man Safety Cars. It also became obvious to most Jaxsons that the lion's share of growth was now coming from the Brooklyn and Riverside routes. Service on the First Street and Walnut Street Loops were being consolidated for efficiency.

The biggest news of the year was the announcement of the Murray Hill Heights Car Line, which by mid-August was blazing a trail southwest of downtown. There was a double inducement to get the line to Murray Hill Heights up and running.

The City of South Jacksonville Muni's new Birney Safety Cars rolled out of the St. Louis plant in two models. These beauties had their photos featured in street railway publications advertising the new products. *Courtesy of Washington University in St. Louis.*

The Jacksonville Development Company had sold some $200,000 in prime building lots in the new addition, and several miles of tree-shaded paved streets were already in place, along with a mammoth artesian water supply, sewer and other utilities, which were expected to be on line shortly. Twenty bungalows of "attractive design" would be completed around the first of the year.

The second big inducement was the relocation of the Florida Military Academy to the Jacksonville area, specifically in Murray Hill Heights. The academy had been heavily recruited by the City of Jacksonville, but they informed the city that they would not build the prestigious educational facility without direct access to a streetcar line. The streetcar company had no interest in such an extension until the school reached a point far enough advanced to support it. After a somewhat protracted dog-and-pony show during which nearly ten years elapsed, the stars finally aligned and all three projects got on the map.

Originally known as the Lemon Street Line (today's College Street), the line ran from the end of Myrtle Avenue to Edison, to Dellwood, to Margaret, to Myra, to Stockton, to College, across the ACL Railroad Tracks and proceeded to Edgewood via Plymouth Street.

By August 1923, the poles had been set, and grading was moving at a lively pace. Tracks were already in place along Date (Edison) and Banana (Dellwood), and the company was using electric welders for bonding wires. Interestingly, there is no mention of installation of the all-critical "diamond" (aka crossover, a piece of special track work where one railroad line crosses another at grade) where the traction company passed over the Atlantic Coast Line Railroad. Diamonds are relatively high-maintenance items and, both historically as well as contemporarily, are often the source of prodigious legal affrays and monumental liabilities.

Once again, a year would close out on a sour note; a public mass meeting to protest a fare increase congealed into a permanent organization to resist any future increases in streetcar fares. Thus, Telfair Stockton, the man who had been so instrumental in the building up of the streetcar system, was elected chairman of the new committee in the city council chambers. A meeting and public rally was scheduled for Tuesday, December 11, and "vigorous speeches" were a promised inducement to those who would attend.

Former city councilman A.E. Adamson, the committee's secretary, said that the traction company's annual revenue with the seven-cent fare was averaging around $1 million per year. "If they get the ten-cent fare we expect them to ask for, it means the citizens of the city will be paying the traction company an additional $600,000 per annum—no small matter to the working class of our city."

The committee promised it was prepared to take all the necessary steps to oppose the traction company and had every confidence in the bitter fight that was still to come. The State Railroad Commission was coming to town for a hearing on the fare increase on Monday the seventeenth, and as usual, the Stone and Webster people were well prepared for the fight. The would-be combatants were also ready to "go around the barn" a few times over the company's desire to replace streetcars in Oakland.

At the end of 1923, the City of South Jacksonville opened bids for $100,000 in streetcar bonds, the genesis of the transcendently named City of South Jacksonville Municipal Railways (the South Jax Muni).

On Thursday, May 15, 1924, the sister cities of Jacksonville and South Jacksonville held a cyclopean celebration of unity, the bonding mortar provided by steel rails. The inauguration of the Muni was marked by a day of festivities and ceremonies. A parade of twelve streetcars and over one hundred automobiles and parade floats all decorated with bunting, flags and banners made a trip that started in South Jacksonville with the three new Muni-owned streetcars leading the way and eight Jacksonville Traction cars loaned for the occasion. The cars were completely jam-packed with merrymakers as they traversed the lines of the new system offering free rides. When the Muni cars reached the top of the bridge, they were met by more Jacksonville Traction cars. Mayor John T. Alsop Jr. of Jacksonville and Mayor William P. Belote of South Jacksonville posed for photos with a symbolic clasping of hands lasting a full minute, whilst the siren of South Jacksonville and the heavy voice of "Big Jim," the steam whistle at the Jacksonville municipal power plant, were enjoined by dozens of other whistles, bells, horns and noise makers all along the waterfront.

Slowly rolling northward, the Jacksonville Traction cars were now in the lead and bringing up the rear, with the new Muni cars sandwiched in the middle. Over the bridge, turning right onto the viaduct and again on Bay Street, the parade continued to Laura, where it turned north to Forsyth, to Main and back to Bay, slowly returning to the bridge. This was the route that all future South Jacksonville–Jacksonville cars would follow. Scores of shoppers, dockworkers, office workers and other employees stayed behind after normal business hours in both cities to watch this memorable odyssey.

Mr. Paul Marion, president of the South Jacksonville City Council, presided over the ceremonies, adding more tidbits of truth about fixed-rail transit as factual then as it is today: "None of us can accurately estimate the marvelous results which will accrue from the streetcar line." Marion then introduced Mayor Alsop of Jacksonville, who said, "I bring you greetings of the best city on earth, the metropolis of the greatest state in the Union." Alsop continued, "It was I that had the honor of typewriting the charter under which the City of South Jacksonville as a municipality now exists. It was seventeen years ago when I was secretary to the present judge H.B. Philips, chairman of the State Road Department, who was a South Jacksonville resident at that time." Alsop commended the traction company and the Muni for taking two sister cities and welding them into one large community, a marriage that could only be accomplished with the sounds of the ring of steel. "I remember when there was some talk in Jacksonville of annexing South Jacksonville, but if your growth continues at the pace it has during the past two years, we in Jacksonville had better look to our laurels, lest you consider annexing us," said Alsop.

Telegrams and letters of congratulations were received from various officials including Governor Cary A. Hardee, Judge Philips of the State Road Department and from St. Augustine city manager Eugene Masters. These items were unanimous in voicing sincere joy in the accomplishments of the two cities and regret that events, as they were, did not permit them to attend the opening.

For the purpose of souvenirs, fares were instituted when the grand procession made the return trip to South Jacksonville. The very first fare-paying passenger on the South Jacksonville Muni was one Harry O. Turner, who lived at the foot of Forrest Street in South Jacksonville. Mr. George Prescott, of the Jacksonville Traction Company, was the operator who vended the first fare. In the first full day of fare-paying operation, the South Jacksonville Muni earned $117, representing some 1,617 rider trips.

In a show of solidarity when the company went to a new system of unlimited-ride weekly passes, Mayor Alsop of Jacksonville paid $1.25 for system pass number one, and Mayor Belote of South Jacksonville purchased pass number two. For Jacksonville and South Jacksonville, the new passes ushered in the new fare structure, which was approved over the howls of many prominent citizens, and the council's select "committee on death to all fare increases." Five tokens were available for thirty-five cents; school fares would remain unchanged; and the new straight fare went for ten cents per trip.

In the summer of 1925, the employees held a grand picnic at Panama Park, and no doubt John Ingle talked up the sweeping improvements that the company was working on that were scheduled to take effect on September 20.

For several months now in 2014, we've been hearing about an efficient "new" bus transit system in the city. It is expected that by the end of the year, sweeping changes will tighten up headways on the various routes to as little as twenty minutes, give or take. Funny, in 1925, the streetcars were moving from a "deplorable system of ten- to sixteen-minute headways." It was expected that by the end of the year, sweeping changes would tighten up the headways on the various lines to as little as five to six minutes. Some of the highlights were for the Murray Hill cars to operate on seven-and-a-half-minute headways; every other car would turn back at the railroad crossing on College, giving the Edgewood/Military Academy fifteen-minute headways. Florida Avenue/LaVilla cars would maintain eleven-minute headways. Riverside, Avondale, Main, Pearl and Walnut Street Fairfield/Union Station car lines ran on six-minute headways. The Brentwood Line would no longer make the trip from Main and Bay to Union Station; instead it would run a loop at the foot of Main, using Ocean and Forsyth, thus cutting the headways to twelve minutes. The Enterprise Line would use Hogan, Beaver and Laura to loop back, closing those headways to twelve minutes. Kings Avenue Line would also tighten to a twelve-minute schedule.

If this leaves you, my gentle reader, in the dark, consider that the Number 1 and 2 lines of the New York Metropolitan Transit Authority Subways run on four- to six-minute headways in 2014, something Jacksonville Traction achieved in 1925.

Manager Triay, of the Jacksonville Traction Company passed away, and John P. Ingle succeeded him as the new "brass hat,"[20] in April 1925.

Suddenly, the Great Florida Boom was over. In 1925, *Forbes Magazine* warned that workers were being laid off in south Florida, while the number of real estate salespeople was still increasing. Before the October 29, 1929 stock market crash brought down the rest of the nation, Florida was feeling the pain.

In May 1925, the City of South Jacksonville announced that its streetcar system earned a 10 percent profit in its first fiscal year. The people of South Jacksonville were largely celebrating their success story, and the local newspapers reported glowing accounts of the mood in the little borough, as it was one of the few such utility investments, private or public, to actually make a profit in the first year of operation. Tracks were then pushed out across the Florida East Coast Railway mainline on Atlantic to Times Square, where they connected with the Mayport branchline. The original issue for building the line had been $100,000, but the actual system came in $37,000 less than expected, allowing for additions both to the east and southward into San Jose. The six cars of the little pike were operated by the Jacksonville Traction Company with four in daily service and two reserved for students going to school in Jacksonville. The Muni ran the cars on thirteen-minute headways, meaning even in this small area, a streetcar was literally almost always in sight.

Stone and Webster delivered a large fleet of some thirty six One-Man Birney Safety Cars during this season and immediately began to see an improvement in accident rates over the older, larger two-man cars. This was largely attributed to the custom of the day of jumping onto moving cars, catching the lower step or occasionally missing the lower step, leading to serious bodily injuries. The change in configuration made this impossible, and the single operator of both the car and the door eliminated many of the human-error accidents. Brill Car Company built most of this final order of new cars, and the balance came from the American Car Company. The safety benefit was just one bonus; the other was the phase out of conductors on the cars, making for a much more economical operation.

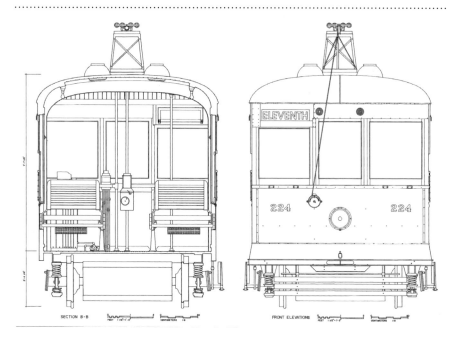

Courtesy of the University of Arkansas and the Historic American Engineering Record, National Park Service, Delineated by Bert V. Calhoun II.

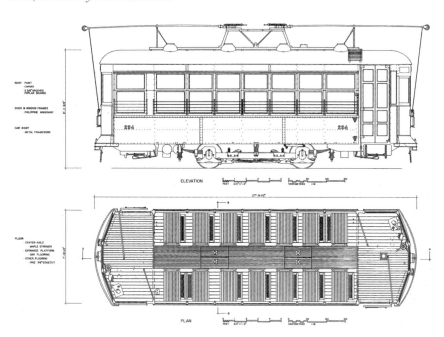

Courtesy of the University of Arkansas and the Historic American Engineering Record, National Park Service, Delineated by Bert V. Calhoun II.

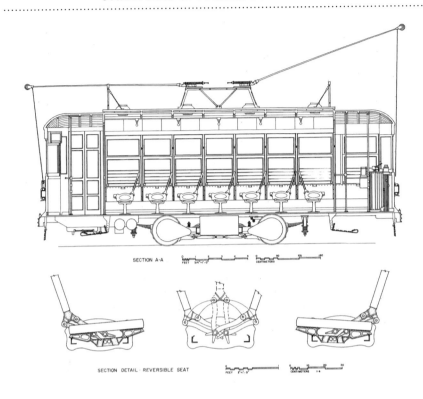

SECTION A-A

SECTION DETAIL · REVERSIBLE SEAT

This Birney Safety Car 224 (also shown on the previous page) operating in downtown Fort Smith, Arkansas, is a virtual twin to the Jacksonville and South Jacksonville fleet. These drawings give us a look "under the hood." *Courtesy of the University of Arkansas and the Historic American Engineering Record, National Park Service, Delineated by Bert V. Calhoun II.*

South Jacksonville's Birneys large and small became stars as their images were used to promote the economical new cars around the world. *Courtesy of Washington University in St. Louis.*

HERE'S YOUR CHANCE TO WIN A PRIZE—AND AT THE SAME TIME HELP US CHOOSE THE BEST COLOR OR COLORS TO REPAINT OUR STREET CARS—YOUR STREET CARS

ANNOUNCING

A

Street Car Painting
CONTEST
by the

JACKSONVILLE TRACTION COMPANY
J P INGLE, Manager

The aggrieved company continued to reach out to the community. *Florida Times-Union* advertisement. *From the author's collection.*

Both the Lake Shore and the San Jose Developments instituted new bus service directly from downtown to the heart of the developments. Following on the heels of the Lake Shore bus developments, Murray Hill asked for additional bus service, which of course was provided by the Jacksonville Traction Company. In fact, by February 7, 1928, a league of citizens asked for additional bus services to many of the newer neighborhoods where the company had been want to lay new track. None of this was foreign to the traction company, as Stone and Webster also owned the Florida Motor Lines, a statewide bus system that would become the cornerstone of Southeastern Greyhound Lines.[21]

"Phantasmagoria! A Chromatic Orgy!" Thus shouted the headlines and newsboys from every corner of the city in the summer of 1928. Starting on

April 9, one of the last great happy events bonding the Jacksonville Traction Company with the citizens of the city was the brilliant idea of a coloring contest. Starting the previous month, the traction company had offered over $100 in prizes to schoolchildren who would color a streetcar drawing that ran in the local papers. There was a $25 grand prize and lesser prizes down to $1. The winners would see real streetcars painted in their personal designs, and the city, at least temporarily, was afflicted with "trolley mania."

One of the local papers teased, "You had better dig out those old smoked glasses you used for that last solar eclipse. Or else carry a pair of specs with a deep violet tinge to save your eyes. Put 'em in your pocket because today or tomorrow or sometime within the near future you may need them…Sooner or later you'll cross ITS trail…It's a streetcar." They went on to explain that soon "it" would have brothers and sisters and aunts and uncles running all over the city. Mr. John P. Ingle nicknamed the first product of the youthful designers and the shop crews "Painters' Colic."

12
CALL OF THE CUCKOO

The fun started coming to a close in 1928, when the city presented a proposed new franchise to Jacksonville Traction. Nieuport B. Estes, of Georgia-Florida Motor Lines, presented a franchise offer to the city in which the company promised to replace the entire streetcar system with a "modern, flexible bus system." Estes said he had $750,000 dollars of backing to invest in the new system and made the dubious claim of superior service and promised the fare would not exceed ten cents. Estes Company belonged to C.B. Warner, and Warner owned the entire bus service in Cincinnati. The bus system in Cincinnati was involved in the National City Lines Great Streetcar Conspiracy, which was funded by General Motors, Standard Oil, Firestone, Phillips 66, Twin-Coach and a host of smaller investors within the highway industry. Many of the city councilmen were swayed into believing that the new package would enhance the bottom line; after all, the new company promised to bring in a "professional transportation director" who would work directly with the city to provide for all of Jacksonville's needs. In addition, the bus company told the council that it "believed every corporate citizen should pay taxes." However, Mayor Alsop stepped in and vetoed any taxation on bus transit in Jacksonville; the streetcars were not so lucky. So with the mayor saying no taxes for buses, and the bus company saying they should pay taxes, the opinion of the public began to shift. Little did anyone suspect the city of Jacksonville was about to be "taken for a ride" in a most literal way.

The man who worked and saved and bought his own car deserves the privacy he pays for.
Let's discourage hitch-hiking!

Jacksonville Traction Company

J. P. Ingle, Manager

Facing a precipitate end, the company launched a series of informative ads. *Florida Times-Union* advertisement. *From the author's collection.*

The most prosperous section of any town is on or near the transportation lines.

Let's discourage hitch-hiking! It takes business away from the electric railway and bus lines which build property values.

Florida Times-Union advertisement. From the author's collection.

Charles Kettering, a Loudonville, Ohio native and vice-president of General Motors, was closely associated with Flxible for almost the entire first half of the company's existence. In 1914, Flxible was incorporated with the help of Kettering, who then became president of the company and joined the board of directors.

Not exactly helping the cause of rail transit, the street railway took delivery of what the newspapers called the "new streetcars." A small fleet of forty-passenger, blue and cream colored Twin-Coaches was delivered for new services to Avondale and Murray Hill. Twin-Coach was ultimately sold to Flxible.

Mayor Alsop said the buses were okay, and the ride was unexpectedly smooth. The new bus line shaved twenty minutes off the previous shuttle bus, and free rides were given during the weekend. As a harbinger of things to come, the new schedule "featured" twenty-minute peak and thirty-minute off-peak headways. The bus ride cost ten cents or a token and three cents; no school passes were accepted, but transfers to all car lines were issued except for the Murray Hill streetcar line.

To further the bad luck, January 20, 1929, dawned very foggy—visibility was nearly zero. A Florida East Coast Railway train was switching at Merrill-Stevens Shipyard. As the tracks ended at the river, all of the action took place back and forth across Atlantic Boulevard. A watchman protected the crossing at Atlantic.

The watchman at Atlantic claimed he signaled the crossing and that a streetcar ran over the signal, but the streetcar operator saw it differently. "The lantern was lit and sitting on the ground next to the watchman's shanty where it usually is when he is inside. I got to the center of the track when the end of a twenty-five-car string of boxcars loomed out of the fog. All I could do was put on full power and we almost cleared the track when the boxcar slammed into us. If the watchman was there, we didn't see him." The South Jacksonville Muni streetcar, valued at $14,000, was hurled sixty-five feet down the track and more or less folded around a corner of a boxcar—a total loss. The engineer of the train had no idea anything had happened until he was finally able to see a signal.

Harry Simmons, a twenty-nine-year-old mechanic from Spring Park, saw the boxcar and dove out of the car in a panic; as a result, he was crushed to death. The operator stood at his controller and received a nasty back injury. Another passenger was said to be in shock, while a couple others had bumps and bruises. The incident didn't endear the streetcar operation to the media.

The Jacksonville Union Terminal had expanded to handle five thousand passengers per hour on some twenty-five hourly trains. Needless to say, that beehive of urban activity was the primary stop on the street railway system. This was to be expected in a city where a resident transportation "expert" explained to the newspapers that the automobile was just a fad and would soon fade from the scene. As proof, he stated that horses and mules were still largely popular and that Jacksonville certainly wasn't in the motor age yet.

The city council was guilty of piling on, and in April, it informed the traction company that if it didn't double track the entire Main Street Line, it would revoke the franchise in sixty days. The threat was expected to scare the traction company into immediate compliance, though no councilman would admit that he would sponsor such a repealing ordinance. John Ingle stated that the patronage on the Springfield–Main Street lines didn't warrant double track. At the end of June, the company renewed serious efforts to convince the newly installed city council to renew its franchise.

The first hearing on the new franchise was held in October. The threat was revoked when Ingle appeared before the council and explained that the new trackage would cost $36,000, and in any case, the rails could not be obtained within the deadline. Still, the company agreed to build twenty-two new concrete "safety island" type stops along Bay Street, designed to route automobile traffic safely around the stops, and the city dropped the double track demand. On May 29, the city council repealed a new franchise offer, saying the company wasn't living up to the obligations it demanded.

The eradicators continued their work; meanwhile, a new study was published for the city. The various traction companies were innocently buying in and expanding the bottom line of the General Motors–National City Lines Cartel. In 1920, only 16 traction companies operated supplemental bus service, but by 1928, some 361 were offering these exhaust-spewing vehicles. In 1925, the traction companies purchased 2,660 buses, and by 1929, that number swelled to 10,733 nationally; so said the report. The cartel continued that the average passenger automobile carried 1.25 people and occupied 84 square feet of pavement or 67 square feet per passenger of paving surface, and the average streetcar occupies only 250 square feet of pavement or 11 square feet per passenger of paving surface.

from Mules to Electric Cars and Motor Buses

50 Years of Progress

THANKS FOR YOUR PATIENCE!

Depression has levied heavily against the income of all street car companies. Regardless of the loss of revenues, the Jacksonville Traction Company has maintained its schedules and service without interruption and at a large loss to its stockholders.

The Traction Company is most grateful to the people of Jacksonville for their patience during the trials that have beset the company the past several years, and the company will shortly be in a position to justify the faith the people have placed in it.

Present plans call for new equipment, new extensions and many improvements, to be undertaken during the coming year.

ANNIVERSARIES remind us that 52 years have passed since Jacksonville had its first street railway transportation. That consisted of two or three crude cars drawn by plodding mule

Now Jacksonville boasts of a modern street railway an bus system reaching into every part of the city, a system tha will compare favorable with any of its size in the United State

Many millions of dollars have been invested during th past 50 years in tracks, pavements and rolling equipment,—i vested by the several owners of the system in the faith that Jac sonville would some day be a great city.

The companies operating this system have seen good yea and bad, but during all the years, they have strived to give t people the best service possible at the lowest possible fare.

Essential to Jacksonville's continued growth is her str transportation system. Help the Traction Company serve Ja sonville better by "using the street cars."

JACKSONVILLE TRACTION COMPANY

The excruciated traction company took out full-page ads to plead its case in the local papers. A fare hike allowed it to pay its operating costs but there was nothing left to pay down $1 million in debit, and the banks would not extend credit. Then the city hit the company with a $100,000 bill for paving and sewers on Main Street. *From the* Times-Union/Jacksonville Journal, *author's collection.*

Opposite: There were only two car lines and only eight streetcars still operating when this Brobdingnagian Kings Road Turtleback was photographed next to its paltry ruination, and this Edison Avenue–Union Station bus has already replaced the Seaboard–Lackawanna Shops streetcar line. Times-Union *photo, courtesy of the Jacksonville Historical Society.*

With amazing perception, the reported streetcars would continue to be a critical transit need. General Motors and National City Lines concluded that buses serve two primary functions: as an express medium from outlying points to the urban core and as feeders to streetcar lines. The latter was considered exceptionally promising.

At this point, however, the report strayed in a diametrically opposite direction from contemporary thought and practice. It suggested that bus lines should take over the longer rail lines—Norwood, Panama, Ortega and North Shore—on a local schedule to within a fifteen- to twenty-minute zone from the core and hence operate as nonstop expresses on into the central city. This, the report said, would allow General Motors and National City Lines to pull up the tracks beyond the fifteen- to twenty-minute zones. The report suggested eliminating the Ortega Line beyond Fairfax and the Eighth Street Line entirely, including both the Talleyrand extension as well as the Evergreen–Phoenix Line. The new suggested system would affect the following lines:

LINE	DAILY ROUND TRIPS	HEADWAYS IN MINUTES
Avondale–Main Street	109	9.25/morning and 7.5/evening
Avondale Brentwood	17	12 (night only)
Brentwood	84	11
Depot–Fairfield	101	11
Enterprise	73	15
Florida Avenue–La Villa	65	18
Kings Road	78	15
Lackawanna	89	15
Murray Hill	94	13/morning and 11/evening
Ortega	51	30
Phoenix Park	75	15
South Jacksonville	75	16
Walnut–Pearl	114	10.5
Talleyrand–Meets	72	15
Myrtle Avenue–Oakland	52	20

In November 1930, the *Jacksonville American* newspaper launched its anti-streetcar campaign: "Railroads and Buses Vie for Preferment; Motor Transport Heads Say R.R.'s Trying to Gobble All the Business." Thus, it was tactfully swaying public opinion, while engaging in the same practice. Meanwhile, Florida's counties and cities as well as the federal government were pouring millions of tax dollars into massive road-building projects. The electric railways were paying taxes for franchises, real estate and income, in addition to road paving, street sweeping, operations, maintenance and landscaping costs.

The Florida East Coast Railroad paid $2,500,000 annually to the state. However, the *American* claimed it was really "only" $1,553,558.77, or 8.4 percent of its valuation, and accused the railroad of deception. While accusing the street railways and railroads of propaganda, the article went on to claim that buses were being charged 760 percent of their valuation, which of course would be an insurmountable obstacle to profitability.

The primary clue that GM's conspirators had a hand in this publication was a claim of "legislative oppression" of the automotive industry. "Pleasure car owners in Florida pay the highest license and gasoline tax in the United States," was the call to citizens to enjoin the battle.

The next step in the *Jacksonville American*'s campaign zeroed in on the Jacksonville Traction Company. In the articles titled "Franchise Delay Injurious to City," and "Time Has Come for Council to Take a Stand and Issue Ultimatum," it explained that the company was the largest taxpayer in the city, paying some $75,000 annually and that the company could no longer afford to pay the annual franchise tax of $30,000. The *American* said the city council should say to the company, "Gentlemen, for nearly two years we have been trying to write a franchise that would be acceptable to you. The time is drawing near when the interests of the city demand that a satisfactory transportation franchise shall be negotiated with some concern to be in effect immediately upon the expiration of your present franchise in 1932. Here are our terms. Accept them or leave them." The ante was raised when it said no city could long thrive without quality transportation and that the street railways' expansions had come to a standstill, and its equipment and track were rapidly deteriorating. Thus, the highway boys had thrown down the gauntlet.

In still another article, Nieuport B. Estes wrote, "Working through their employees the railroad company's operation out of Jacksonville are engaged in a campaign to discredit and boycott the bus and truck lines." Estes wrote, "We do not censure railway employees who lend themselves to such a campaign. Doubtless they believe what they have been told by their employers, namely, that the bus and truck are responsible for the decline in railway revenue." The immediate take-away from this statement was if it's not the buses, it is obviously because railways are inferior, exactly the message General Motors, National City Lines and Nieuport Estes were conspiring to push. Perhaps the best clue is that another Estes, Elliott M. Estes, a GM engineer, would eventually be rewarded with the position of CEO of the corporation on October 1, 1974.

On October 10, 1931, the *Jacksonville American* proudly announced, "Local Interests May Control Streetcars," but as we have seen, the cabal was in this up to their necks. "Of particular interest to streetcar patrons is the proposal to abandon car lines and substitute buses." Further commentary stated,

The company doesn't propose to make any further extensions of its tracks. When extension of service is necessary it shall be by bus. As the company abandons streetcars for other forms of transportation, it agrees to take up its tracks and re-surface the streets where the rails have lain.

It is now clear that the Traction Company has suffered severely, not only as a result of the depression, but more particularly from the increasing

VOTE Tues. March 29
For New
TRACTION FRANCHISE

Go to the polls Tuesday and cast your ballot for the better transportation service you've been wanting.

City Council has granted a new franchise to the Jacksonville Traction Company in which the city's interest and yours as a citizen are carefully protected. The traction company has accepted this franchise. But you, the voters, must give your final approval of it at the polls Tuesday.

Approval of the franchise is a vital matter touching the comfort, convenience and protection of every citizen of Jacksonville. It also affects Jacksonville's growth as a city for the reason that no city can develop and expand without adequate public transportation facilities.

Every man, woman and child who uses the traction company's facilities regularly or occasionally is directly concerned with this new franchise and the improved service it will bring. Every one who can vote should vote—for the franchise.

Read this list for specific information:

1. Who Can Vote? Every person who was qualified to vote in the last general election may vote in the franchise election without further registration or payment of poll tax.

2. Will The Franchise Affect Fares? No! There will be no change in fares, weekly passes, school tickets or transfers under the new franchise. City Council has carefully guarded your interests against any unfavorable change in fares or service. Firemen, policemen and city health department employes will be carried free as heretofore.

3. Why do Service Improvements Have to Wait on the New Franchise? Because a franchise is simply a permit from the city to the Jacksonville Traction Company to operate in Jacksonville for a period of years. Until the franchise is granted, any expenditure for new equipment and improved service would be as uncertain an investment as construction of a building on land you do not own or hold under lease for a term of years.

4. How do Mayor Alsop and City Council President Adams Feel About the Franchise? The favorable opinions of these two city executives are emphatically expressed in their letters appearing on this page.

WHERE TO VOTE

Go to your regular ward or ward-precinct polling place to cast your ballot. The election will be exactly like any general city election. Here is a list of polling places in the various wards:

Ward	Place
1-A	Third and Walnut Streets.
1-B	47 East Eighth Street.
2	226 Florida Avenue.
3	Old Armory, Forsyth and Market Streets.
4	11 East Adams Street.
5	210 West Adams Street.
6-A	1608 Main Street.
6-B	2021 Pearl Street.
7	408 West Forsyth Street.
8-A	908 West Adams Street.
8-B	2097 Edison Avenue.
9-A	403 Park Street.
9-B	562 Riverside Avenue.
10-A	2218 Oak Street.
10-B	2731 College Street.
10-C	1017 Edgewood Avenue.
10-D	875 Stockton Street.
11	Fourth Street and Evergreen Ave.
12-A	2416 Phoenix Avenue.
12-B	Boy Scouts Hall, Buffalo Avenue.
13-A	Sixty-third and Main Streets.
13-B	Woodbine and Perry Streets.
13-C	6201 Norwood Avenue.
14-A	2980 Thomas Street.
14-B	611 McDuff Avenue.
15-A	1262 McDuff Avenue.
15-B	3643 St. Johns Avenue.
16-A	2906 Corinthian Street.
16-B	Ferris Building, Lake Shore Drive.
17	10 W. St. Johns Ave., So. Jax.
18	Community Bldg., San Marco Blvd., South Jax.

TO THE PEOPLE OF JACKSONVILLE:

If it is true that "out of much discussion cometh knowledge", then surely the citizens of Jacksonville are quite conversant with the terms of the street car franchise recently passed by the City Council and whole heartedly approved by me as mayor.

Notwithstanding these many discussions and the very serious consideration of the franchise covering a period of more than five years, the franchise cannot become effective until approved by the people, which, in my opinion, is a very proper and just provision of the law.

In my opinion, the right to vote on all questions is one of the most precious privileges given us under our Constitution.

Yours very truly,
(Signed) John T. Alsop, Jr.,
Mayor

TO THE PEOPLE OF JACKSONVILLE:

It is my earnest hopes that the voters of Jacksonville will go to the polls Tuesday, March 29, and vote FOR the new traction franchise.

As you know, the franchise is the result of many months of work and study on the part of the City Council and its legal advisors. I feel that the franchise is entirely fair in every way to the Jacksonville Traction Company. I KNOW that it fully protects the interests of the city and the taxpayers.

Under this franchise which is, in effect, permission by the city for the Jacksonville Traction Company to continue operations here, the company will, at last, be able to begin the service improvements it has so long contemplated but has been unable to begin until the Jacksonville Traction Company has had assurance of renewal of its operating contract with the city.

I have no doubt whatever that the election will show an overwhelming approval of the franchise.

Desperate for survival, the tormented JTCO gave the new franchise its best shot. *From the author's collection.*

competition of the motor car and the demands for more modern facilities and better service [even though the streetcars were running on twelve to fifteen-minute headways]. *It cannot hope, it is said, to pay out under its present capitalization and its only salvation lies in such a re-organization as has been suggested.*

Finally, it was all over for Jacksonville's streetcars. In early January 1932, the *Jacksonville Journal* and the *Times-Union* announced, "The Car Company is Sold to the Motor Transit Company for $335,000." The bondholders read newspapers, too, and they decided to foreclose on the first mortgages of the Jacksonville Traction Company's entire properties. The traction company finally succumbed to mounting pressure to go out of existence. The new franchise had a teaser that it would operate over any new route the city council requested and a stick that the streetcar system was frozen; no extensions could be made, and the cars were to be scrapped. Bustitution had come to Jacksonville, along with all of the promises of better service and a permanent ten-cent fare. Looking back from the twenty-first century, with buses running on thirty-, forty-five- and sixty-minute headways and fares of $1.50 or more, it's easy to see how we were "taken for a ride."

Shortly after the sale was finalized on January 13, 1932, the *Jacksonville Journal* reported that "Jacksonville is Center for General Motors Sales." It seems that the General Motors Sales Company immediately chose Jacksonville as one of three centers of operation and distribution in the southeast. Florida, Georgia, Alabama, Tennessee and North and South Carolina would be eating out of Jacksonville's hands. As the wholesale distribution center for Cadillac, LaSalle, Buick, Oldsmobile and Pontiac, the rewards for Bustitution were rich indeed.

Though county commissioner St. Elmo Acosta had never given up on his electric line to the beach, he tried one more time in 1931, just as all of the attacks on street railways were heating up. This time, Acosta had a new twist; he pushed for electric trolley buses on a one-hundred-foot strip between downtown and the beaches. He had the plan all worked out, right down to the pricing and landscaping. Once again, Acosta's pleas and urgings fell on deaf ears.

Heaping insult on injury, the Florida East Coast Railroad ended service to the Jacksonville Beaches and announced that the thirty-four-mile Mayport Line would be abandoned as soon as a disposition of the materials could be determined. So 1932 ended in a double loss for Jacksonville's city builders.

The dominos fell one by one. The Enterprise and Beaver Street car lines went down in 1933. The Edison–Lackawanna Line vanished on May 19, 1936.

Following on the heels of the sale came a reward and certificate designating the Motor Transit Company as the outstanding large-city

The Motor Transit Company executives were celebratory on that gloomy December day when much of downtown stood in the rain to watch the final run as if attending a funeral for a friend. Times-Union *photo, courtesy of the Jacksonville Historical Society.*

service company in the United States, signed by the leadership of the National Association of Motor Bus Operators and the managing director of the American Transit association.

Bustitution continued, and it was announced that the streetcars would run their last miles amidst farewell ceremonies as soon as a new batch of the latest modern buses arrived. The final regular streetcar service was on the evening of December 12, on the last two surviving lines—La Villa and Kings Road—and they were operating from a pool of only eight active cars where once there had been well over one hundred.

On an appropriately freezing cold, rainy December 13, 1936, the streetcars abdicated their throne—according to the paper, "forever." Invited dignitaries lined up and stood in the rain awaiting the final cars in front of city hall at the corner of Forsyth and Ocean Streets. The company announced that with the complete motorization of the system, it would shortly institute sweeping changes (an understatement if there ever was one). Judge Barrs, a two-term city councilman who would go on to serve thirty-six years on the bench,[22] paid the last fare, and G.D. Gay, a longtime resident and a man who had ridden the first electric car on the Jacksonville Street Railway, was also among the passengers. The whole group was taken around the loop to Bay Street and then over the viaduct to the carbarn in Riverside. Hundreds of citizens stood in the pouring rain along the sidewalks to bid the cars a fond and sad farewell. Mr. Gabe Bonds, a forty-year employee of the traction company, perhaps summed it up best when he commented, "One day the king quits his job, and the next day I'm just about worked out of a job by these streetcars quitting their jobs."

13
LEAVE 'EM LAUGHING

The extirpation of the American street and interurban railways was the result of devious planning and execution by a cadre of automakers, bus manufacturers, the petroleum industry and shady politicians.[23] The sales pitch was slick, new versus old, flexible versus fixed, "*free*way" versus railway, cheap versus a perception of expensive.

There were a few logical business reasons for the streetcars' demise; most systems were built in the 1890s and were due for major rehabilitation by the 1920s. The cities and states continued to tax the railways, using that income to build a competing highway system. There were no federal, state or local subsidies for capital or operating expenses. Fares were regulated to a minimum, and the regulators required that the companies themselves pay for hearings and elections necessary to raise fares. Transit operators calculated that an uncrowded highway network would allow them to improve services.

What wasn't apparent, at least at first, was what would happen when "new" became "old" again. No one foresaw the bus company bankruptcies and consequential mass dumping of these bus operations onto the public sector.

With time, it would also become apparent that "flexible" isn't flexible if there isn't a roadway to drive on. The public, long since sold on an imagined need for an ever-expanding road and highway system, didn't notice the hidden cost of this sweeping change in mass transit. Further, flexible was a great sales angle until urban planners noticed that large development projects tend to cluster around fixed transportation

An idyllic photo as this large Turtleback rounds the Eleventh and Pearl Street loop. *Courtesy of the Jacksonville Historical Society.*

infrastructure. It is entirely possible for a bus system to attract transit-oriented development (TOD), but there is no question that a rail system is development-oriented transit.

The fact that freeways are not free shouldn't surprise the most hardened highway advocate. It might surprise the average citizen to know that the cost of paving and maintaining an ever-expanding highway system is seldom, if ever, mentioned in the cost of bus transit. Hidden within that figure is the relationship between the axle weight and pavement damage, a relationship that is not linear, but exponential. A single axle loaded to forty thousand pounds (twice the legal highway load of twenty thousand pounds per axle) will cause sixteen times more damage than a single axle legally loaded to twenty thousand pounds. According to a Government Accountability Office study, "Excessive Truck Weight: An Expensive Burden We Can No Longer Afford," road damage from one eighteen-wheeler is equivalent to approximately ten thousand cars.

The new (2014) hybrid buses or BRT (Bus Rapid Transit) buses consistently weigh in right at the legal limit of twenty thousand pounds per axle. Considering these heavy vehicles will typically pass over the pavement forty-eight times daily per route, it's no wonder that the various transit agencies don't want to talk about this.

Rail, be it light rail, streetcar, commuter, elevated or subway, has certain built-in economies of longevity unknown to the highway industry; a life expectancy of forty-five years for track is only ten years for roads. Vehicle life expectancy is twenty-five years for rail cars (though many are still operating at fifty, seventy-five and even one hundred years) and from eight to twelve years for buses, though the industry is currently pushing for an eight-year standard. In a word, this should redefine our perception of which mode is "cheap" and which mode is truly "expensive."

Lastly, there are questions of environmental sustainability of the various modes of transportation. No one would argue that the automobile, even if it ran on dirty bathwater and emitted pure mountain air, does anything positive for the environment. In terms of pavement alone, we have already paved the equivalent ground surface of our six northeastern-most states. Detractors claim that a power plant pollutes just as much per passenger trip as does the tail pipe of the family car, but detractors don't want to talk about streetcars running on wind, solar, tidal or hydroelectric power.

The sheer viciousness of the highway transit victory over streetcars becomes more apparent when one realizes that almost immediately after the death of America's rail transit properties, the new bus companies launched a war on taxis. On November 17, 1937, just under a year after the last streetcar, the Motor Transit Company in Jacksonville began a disinformation campaign and lobby effort to sweep the cabs off of the city streets.

Finally in 1946, a former United States Naval officer and electrical engineer named E. Jay Quinby, became concerned about the disappearance of America's rail-transit systems under the influence of petroleum, rubber and highway industries. Quinby, published an exposé using his own funds and addressed it to "The Mayors; The City Manager; The City Transit Engineer; The members of The Committee on Mass-Transportation and The Tax-Payers and The Riding Citizens of Your Community."

Quinby's thirty-six-page thesis began, "This is an urgent warning to each and every one of you that there is a careful, deliberately planned campaign to swindle you out of your most important and valuable public utilities—your Electric Railway System."

The amazing document went on to uncover links between National City Lines[24] (and its subsidiaries) to parent owners Firestone Tires, General Motors, Phillips Petroleum, Standard Oil of California and Mack Trucks. The Motor Transit Company was one of the many related or subsidiary companies and a forerunner of the Greyhound Corporation. The name

Motor Transit Company would reappear in various locations, including the demise of the Jacksonville Traction Company.

Today, the city of Jacksonville is finally coming back to the realization that a fixed-transit system is a virtual requirement for a modern progressive city. Unfortunately, the State of Florida controls the transportation authority and continues to parrot the old Motor Transit line, stuck in another decade. It was forty-five years from the time of the last streetcar until a 1981 plan was presented to reconstruct a small portion of the old system. Had the city acted, it would have been the first to return to a heritage streetcar system. During the time Jacksonville has wasted studying a return, nearly one hundred cities have rebuilt their own systems. Streetcar or light-rail talk, studies or projects are also circulating in both Palatka and St. Augustine, as well as nearby Gainesville, Edgewater, Fort Lauderdale, Miami, Sarasota, Tampa, St. Petersburg, Orlando, Savannah and Atlanta. But talk is cheap, and the metropolis of Jacksonville has become very adept at making studies and talk. Meanwhile, the citizens are left to wonder if the city ever got the memo.

In the 1940s, long after the streetcars' demise, this sign was still on duty in Springfield. *Courtesy of the Florida State Photographic Archives.*

You will realize too late that the electric railway is unquestionably more comfortable, more reliable, safer and cheaper to use than the bus system. But what can you do about it once you have permitted the tracks to be torn up? Who do you think you can find to finance another deluxe transit system for your city?

—E. Jay Quinby, 1946.

Jacksonville's fifth economic disaster had come from Detroit. It was absolute, and the city lost its "mojo," perhaps forever.

PART II

ST. AUGUSTINE

14
PERFECT DAY

ST. AUGUSTINE AND NORTH BEACH RAILWAY COMPANY

The city of St. Augustine had recently recovered from the earthquake of January 13, 1879. While not as severe as the building-smashing quake of 1780, if the tremor shook up the citizenry, it certainly didn't jar their resolve to improve their transportation options.

One of the first urban railways in Florida, and one of four to serve the St. Augustine beaches, was a small narrow-gauge horsecar line that crossed the Tolomato River to the North Beach on a palm piling bridge between years 1880 and 1890. The *Transit Journal* noted in 1889, "The St. Augustine and North Beach Railway Company has had surveys and estimates made for a dummy line, Virgil Powers is interested." Powers served as chief engineer of the South-Western Railroad in Macon, Georgia. Investors from Georgia had arrived on the scene in 1888 to reconstruct the railway to standard gauge, equipping it with a small locomotive and a passenger coach. The "new" St. Augustine and North Beach Railway ran from the old brick Jacksonville, St. Augustine and Halifax River Railroad Station at the west end of Orange Street until shortly after Henry Flagler purchased the railroad on December 31, 1885. Under Flagler's leadership, a new Union Station was built adjacent to Malaga Street, and the tiny North Beach Railway extended its tracks to reach it.

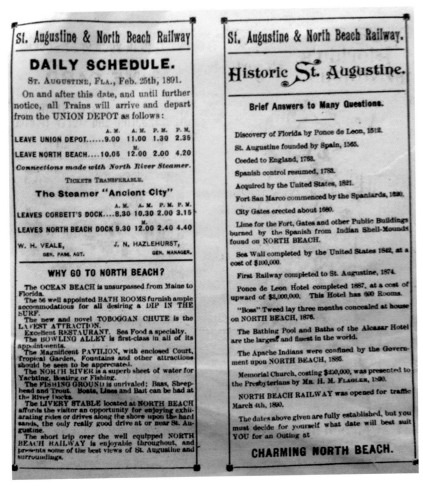

The railway that started it all in the nation's oldest city believed in promotion. *Courtesy of Florida Photographic Archives.*

The little "Dummy Line" followed a path roughly along today's Ponce de Leon Boulevard (U.S. Highway 1) from the depot northward, then angled past the old station by the park and continued straight out across the marsh in a northeasterly direction, clipping the corner of Fort Mose State Park, then crossing the river and the island, arriving near the surf at the current site of the Reef Restaurant. Interestingly, just across the highway from the Reef's parking lot is the North Beach Resort RV park, and down the lane is Aunt Kate's Restaurant, which as of this writing, is still in the hands of one of the original developer families.

The early resort sported a bathhouse, stable, dance pavilion, restaurant, bowling alley and toboggan chute. It was so popular with Flagler's hotel guests that he made an offer to buy the property.

In 1891, the *Transit Journal* reported, "It is stated, on reliable authority, that the North Beach Railway Company are endeavoring to sell their road to H.M. Flagler. The road is nearly three miles in length and originally cost $90,000." Unfortunately for the investment group, the deal didn't go through, as disaster was only four short years away.

In February 1895, the North Beach Resort caught fire and burned to the ground. The railway didn't have insurance coverage enough to rebuild.

In 1900, Frank Usina, a former Flagler employee, and his wife, Kate, moved to the site of the old resort, living in one of the abandoned cabins. Pioneering in a location that wouldn't see electricity until 1940, the Usinas rebuilt a modest version of the resort with a small cash gift from friend Flagler.

Usina constructed a homemade horsecar and reopened the railway, treating guests to fresh seafood cooked over an open fire. The family performed all of the work and even wired up electrical lights using glass-jar batteries. Nevertheless, the little resort proved to be popular once again—popular enough to attract several times the attention of the street railway journals and play a small role in the city's streetcar history.

Paul Capo's Anastasia Island Tramway

Directly across the Matanzas River from St. Augustine is Anastasia Island, and in a day when shoe leather was the primary means of transportation, it presented a much closer alternative to those wishing to spend the day at the beach. The problem was the area between the lighthouse and the foot of the Bridge of the Lions was largely a salt marsh. The salt marshes were a high-tide nursery for sea life and a low-tide hunting ground for the abundant rattlesnakes still present in the local dunes. Paul Capo came along and constructed a small causeway with a tiny narrow-gauge railway using primitive wooden rails. It was, however, his horsecar that allowed people to cross the marsh dry shod and this little nameless tram that first put Anastasia Island on the tourist map.

Paul Capo built a horse-drawn railway over the salt marsh on a long narrow causeway. When the St. Augustine and South Beach Railway came along, Capo moved his "grand conveyance" to North Beach. *Courtesy of the St. Augustine Historical Society.*

St. Augustine and South Beach Railroad and Bridge Company

On May 27, 1886, Captain Allen Wood and Moses Bean incorporated the St. Augustine and South Beach Railroad and Bridge Company. The captain operated a ferry across from the city to the central wharf on the island and calculated that a bridge and a real railroad stood to make him wealthy. The railroad operated as a horsecar line until it acquired a new locomotive, passenger car and one freight car in 1899.

The bridge that was announced in 1892 and completed in 1897 was a long wooden trestle with a center swing span for boat traffic; the railroad was graded and built from the east foot of the bridge to the South Beach. Initially, the tracks did not cross the bridge, and people merely walked across to catch the train for the dune line.

Before the bridge was complete, the new railroad found itself embroiled in a legal battle with the Fish family heirs. Jessie Fish, a pioneer who held claim

The St. Augustine and South Beach Railway was the proverbial chameleon: narrow-gauge, steam-powered, standard-gauge, electric-powered, streetcar, passenger, freight, mail and express line. *Courtesy of the St. Augustine Historical Society.*

to the whole of Anastasia Island, had passed away in 1798, his wife following him in 1825. The ground had lain fallow for four generations when some of Fish's descendants showed up and filed suit, claiming all of the improvements for their own. The case went all the way to the Supreme Court, which took a very dim view of any sudden claims after four generations of neglect and ruled in the railroad's favor.

The Florida State Railroad Commission regulated the freight and passenger tariffs in 1906. A walk across the bridge cost five cents for a pedestrian or bicyclist; twenty-five cents for a two-horse team, wagon and driver, plus five cents for each additional passenger. The train ride from the east end of the bridge to the lighthouse cost fifteen cents, twenty-five cents

St. Augustine & South Beach R'y.

HOURLY TRAIN SERVICE FROM 9.00 A. M. TILL 5.00 P. M , LEAVING . . . .

St. Augustine

ON THE EVEN HOUR, AND

South Beach

ON THE HALF HOUR, STANDARD R. R. TIME, CALLING EACH WAY AT ANASTASIA, THE

Light House and Jetties.

Take the train at east end of Anastasia Bridge for

ANASTASIA VILLAGE.
THE JETTIES, ... 1 Mile.
THE LIGHTHOUSE,
BIRD ISLAND, ... 4 Miles.
JACK MOUND, ...

AND

GREAT SOUTH BEACH,

WHICH IS 5 MILES

Buy all tickets at Bridge Office. The finest picnic groves accessible to St. Augustine.

RAILROAD RATES, INCLUDING BRIDGE.
To Anastasia (Light House), 25c. round trip. To South Beach, 50c. round trip. Above covers all cost, bridge and railroad.

TOLL RATES, BRIDGE ALONE.
Pedestrians or bicyclists, 5c.; horse and rider, 10c.; single buggy or dray, with driver, 15c.; one-horse, 2-seat carriage, with driver, 20c.; double team, with driver, 25c., each additional person, 5c. EACH WAY.

St. Augustine & South Beach R'y.

THE BRIDGE is in the very center of the city, at the foot of King Street.

You can go any way you choose; walk, ride a horse or a bicycle, in a carriage or by train.

BY TRAIN IS A PLEASANT WAY. You walk across the bridge, only 1,900 feet, and at eastern end take passage in a comfortable coach for the Lighthouse Station, called Anastasia, which is one mile, and South Beach Station, which is five miles, and directly on the ocean shore. At South Beach, and also at the Lighthouse Station, there is a

Comfortable Pavilion and Hotel Building,

where you can get a FIRST-CLASS MEAL OR A LUNCH.

Watch the Breakers Roll,
Take a Sea Bath,
Gather Beautiful Shells,
And Ride, Drive or Walk
on the finest Beach in the World.

IF YOU WISH TO DRIVE OR RIDE you may do so entirely away from the train, by the Coquina Quarries, on a natural coquina road, the only one in the world, or by the seashore, on its hard, smooth surface, over fifteen miles of beautiful hard beach, just the place for a wheel or horse.

St. Augustine and South Beach proved to be a railway of perdurability; among the first to arrive, it was also the last to leave. *Courtesy of the St. Augustine Historical Society.*

round trip. From the lighthouse to South Beach likewise cost fifteen cents, twenty-five cents round trip. In doing the math, it's pretty easy to see how a day trip to South Beach could cost an individual fifty-five cents, but some seventeen years later, that same trip was regulated to twenty-five cents round trip, all the way to St. Augustine Beach. Even the much higher earlier fares failed the company, and in the end, maintenance and repairs on a long bridge brought it down, and it filed bankruptcy.

CAPO'S SURFSIDE CASINO AND TRAMWAY

The fourth of the quartet of tiny railways to the beach was again at the behest of Mr. Capo. Capo generally makes a mockery out of the term "taking all of your marbles and going home," as he did exactly that when the new South Beach Railroad put his tiny tram out of business. Capo moved across the bay to the north beach and took his railroad with him. The last of the trams to be built ran from a boat landing where passengers were ferried from the St. Augustine waterfront to Capo's Surfside Casino. The casinos of the day were not actually gambling halls; rather, they were entertainment centers with music, food, sun and dance. Surfside remained popular up until the 1970s, when it was finally torn down and serves today as a beachside park. Its Lilliputian tramway vanished long ago sometime in the intervening period.

ST. AUGUSTINE STREET RAILWAY COMPANY

Not even a rare Florida earthquake could have made a better mess of things than the comedy of bad timing and false starts on the street railway project. As early as June 1884, the progressive citizens of St. Augustine were vociferating for a street railway to call their own. They petitioned the city for tracks on various streets including Cordova, Orange and San Marco (which was called the Shell Road at that time).

On June 25, 1888, the City of St. Augustine signed an ordinance into law granting a twenty-year franchise to the St. Augustine Street Railway Company. The franchise called for tracks to be laid as follows:

Beginning at the basin east of plaza running north on Marine Street, no nearer than six feet of the sea-wall to intersection of same with government reservation near Fort Marion and thence across said reservation (as far as the City of St. Augustine has any authority to make such grant over said reservation said city in no wise warranting the same only giving its consent as far as it is concerned therein) and intersecting with Shell Road north of the city gates and thence north on street known as Shell Road to city limits on the same. Also beginning at western terminus of Orange Street at or near marsh on San Sebastian River running east on said Orange Street and connecting with line on Shell Road north of City Gates; Also to run south from the basin east of plaza on Bay, St. Francis and Marine Street to

Central Avenue thence north on Central Avenue to Bridge Street thence west on Bridge Street to Mill Street; thence north on Mill Street and its extension (should there be any) to Orange Street, and from Mill Street along King Street to western limits of the city.

The handwritten franchise is quite interesting, as it gives us a rare tableau of a burgeoning era. One stipulation was to release the city from opening South Street all the way through to Marine, suggesting that the railway would be an exclusive right of way to complete that line. There were other, more common items in the document, such as the line being of first-class construction, single track, in the street or alongside, but never on the sidewalk. Streetcars were to be electric or horse powered, and they would have rights over all other traffic except fire apparatus. The railway would have to pave the streets up to one foot on each side of its tracks, hold the city harmless in the event of an accident and could charge no more than a five-cent fare. Perhaps the most surprising element was that a stiff fine of up to fifty dollars for blocking the progress of a streetcar could be charged—a great deal of money in those days.

In Ordinance 21 of the the the St. Johns County Ordinances dated July 11, 1889, a franchise was issued to run for thirty years, and the streets over which the line would pass were altered somewhat as follows:

Commencing at the north boundary of the City on San Marco Avenue and running thence south to the city gates, skirting the western and southern boundary of the United States Military Reservation to the sea wall; thence southerly along Bay Street to St. Francis Street; thence on St. Francis Street to Marine Street; thence southerly on Marine Street to South Street; thence westerly on South Street to Central Avenue; thence north on Central Avenue to King Street; thence westerly on King Street to New Augustine: from King Street at its intersection with Malaga Street, north on Malaga Street to Orange Street; thence easterly on Orange Street to the City Gates, and from the intersection of Central Avenue along said Central Avenue south to the city limits, and to and along such other streets of said city as shall be prescribed by ordinance hereafter by said municipality.

This newer ordinance carefully expressed detailed permissions to erect and maintain a powerhouse, poles, wires and other accouterments as may be necessary to power both the cars and illuminate streets, public spaces and residences. This franchise also gave the city the right to buy the electric utility at a price decided on through neutral arbitration.

In 1891, William P. Craig received a contract for the street railway equipment at his office in New York. Order in hand, the gentleman confidently stated that the St. Augustine Street Railway would be in operation by December.

The following year, street railway contractor M.W. Conway of Brooklyn, New York, sailed for St. Augustine, where he was to meet up with both Craig and a gentleman named A.J. Hutchison. Interestingly, this later report stated that the railway actually belonged to Craig, Conway and Hutchison. The company obviously missed its December debut, and it was still talking about how it would spend the winter building out its three-mile road. The *Street Railway Journal* reported that the "line is to be operated for the present with animal power, but the rails will be wired with a view of equipping with electric power in the near future."

Things were running smoothly until the men reached the part addressed in the franchise thusly: "To intersection of same with government reservation near Fort Marion and thence across said reservation (as far as the City of St. Augustine has any authority to make such grant over said reservation said city in no wise warranting the same only giving its consent as far as it is concerned therein)." The newest franchise had required the railway on "written acceptance of said franchise and an acknowledgement, declaration and agreement to construct said railway over the streets hereinbefore mentioned, within sixty days after the passage thereof by the Council," and, needless to say, with the federal delays, there was only so much that could be done.

The government established the first National Military Parks at Chickamauga and Chattanooga in 1890. The ancient Castillo in St. Augustine was still an active military reservation; it had most recently been used as a prison for western Comanche, Kiowa, Arapahoe and Apache Indian warriors and tribal leaders. Plans were already afoot to move the Castillo into a similar park status. Through it all, the military was carefully considering the possibility of allowing the new street railway to cross its reservation.

United States Senate
Washington D.C.
United States Senate Bill S.29
This bill grants a right of way across the southern and western sides of Fort Marion Military Reservation and across the northern end of the

military reservation known as the Powder Magazine lot, in the City of St. Augustine, Florida to the St. Augustine Street Railroad Company. This company is a corporation duly organized under and by virtue of the laws of Florida, and has, by an ordinance of the board of aldermen of St. Augustine, been granted the right to construct and maintain a street railroad in the city and its suburbs for the period of 20 years.

The route of the proposed railway touches the Fort Marion reservation. As this place is of great historic value in being the oldest fort in the United States, and is quite a distance from the city of St. Augustine, and any easy means of transit will prove of great benefit.

The objectionable feature to the bill is the provision granting right of way across the north end of the Powder Magazine lot. This reservation is now too limited for post purposes and it is recommended that the bill be amended so far as right of way over this lot is concerned.

It is also recommended that the Secretary of War may change or remove the tracks on the said reservation whenever in his judgment the interests of the United States require it.

So, as the franchise clock ticked down again and again, other distractions, finances and opportunities presented themselves. Perhaps a problem larger than historic earthquakes or right of ways and forts turning into parks was the smoke rising from revolts against the Spanish Empire in Cuba. These kettles of agitation had been simmering for some time, and by the 1890s, William Hearst and other prominent journalists launched a campaign to defame the Spanish government in any way possible. José Martí came to St. Augustine in the fall of 1892, visiting the grave of Felix Varela, who is buried in the Tolomato Cemetery, and collecting weapons and support for the revolution. Martí was declared the provisional president of the Republic of Cuba and presented with a revolutionary flag while in the city. So as the Senate worked out amendments to the street railway bill, Fort Marion would soon be reinforced in preparation for war with Spain.

The fort served out the war as a military prison and as a mute outpost of the United States Coastal Defense Artillery. In 1900, Fort Marion was established as a United States Park and ultimately a National Monument as the Castillo de San Marcos under the National Park Service.

15

UNACCUSTOMED AS WE ARE

DAFT ELECTRIC RAILWAY

St. Augustine would have to wait for a few more years to join the ranks of electric streetcar cities, though it appears that Dr. Rainey and the Daft Electric Railway established something of a railway in New Augustine. The Daft system, created by inventor Leo Daft, a brilliant contemporary of Thomas Edison and Frank Sprague, was powered by storage batteries. In 1892, it was reported that a Mr. I. Plant had bought the North Beach Railway for $4,000 and that he was expected to buy the St. Augustine Street Railway and merge them into a single operation. A copy of the necessary track changes has been preserved at the St. Augustine Historical Society.

ST. JOHNS LIGHT AND POWER COMPANY, AKA ST. JOHNS ELECTRIC RAILWAY

In 1906, the St. Johns Light and Power Company purchased the assets of the St. Augustine and South Beach Railroad, including the South Beach Resort, and began laying tracks on various streets throughout the city following the customary practice of staying off to the side of the road unless it was necessary to use the traffic lanes. Around Public Square in downtown, the tracks occupied one of today's parking lanes along Avenida Menendez;

The Lilliputian narrow-gauge St. Augustine and South Beach Railway, with its miniature Forney locomotive, stretch 'em out over the salt marshes of Anastasia Island. *Courtesy of the St. Augustine Historical Society.*

the tracks hugged the space between the sea wall and the street. And along Avenidas San Marco and Castillo, it located the railway along the eastern edge of the street, more or less where the sidewalk is today. In October, after exceptionally high tides blown in by a gale-force wind flooded much of the old city and wiped out several hundred feet of the old South Beach Railroad, a crew was put to work to move that track. Prone to frequent tidal interruptions, the South Beach track was shifted off the original roadbed and onto the new road causeway, which allowed the former remaining roadbed to form a bulwark of protection.

The long-awaited approval from the government engineers at the "Reservation" finally arrived in June 1907, permitting the work of building a city system to move forward.

Initially, there was a fuss from Henry Flagler, who threatened to close the Ponce de Leon Hotel if the streetcar line was built past the front door on King

A popular postcard view of St. Augustine's St. Johns Electric Railway. *Courtesy of the St. Augustine Historical Society.*

Street. While the aging hotelier had a certain appetence for streetcars and urban transit, having built several lines in various places himself, he was at first adamant over bells, horns and wires. There was no better route between the railroad station and downtown than King Street. Flagler's intransigence would send St. Augustine's street railway off on another diversion.

In April 1907, with much of the track in place and poles and wires going up throughout the city, the newspaper announced that the company was installing the Maximum Surface Contact System for Electric Traction on both King and Malaga Streets.

The surface contact system eliminated the overhead wires seen in virtually all nostalgic streetcar photos. A conduit was passed along the center of the track, and a series of small metal boxes resting on top of the crossties were spaced at six- to ten-foot intervals. Power passed through the conduit and from box to box. The streetcars were equipped with a magnetized shoe that rode about three inches above the tops of the boxes. As a car passed over a box, an armature was drawn upward by the magnetized shoe on the car, energizing the box and allowing the shoe to make electrical contact with the brass box lid. As soon as the car's shoe passed over the box, contact was broken, and the power was to the box was cut off.

Taken from an incredibly rare print that became an equally obscure postcard, this is the only known photo of a St. Augustine open car in the city. Few of today's tourist trolley tour operators understand or appreciate the numbers of visitors who would gladly ride their trams as they flocked to such a streetcar today. *Courtesy of the St. Augustine Historical Society.*

In theory, it sounded like a foolproof method of energizing the railway and an answer to the company's Flagler conundrum. The problem was that this was very early in the advancement of electric power transmission and technology and the patent for the system was barely a year old. On one quarter-mile-long test track in Williamsport, Pennsylvania, twenty of the contact "studs" had been broken off after a few thousand cars passed over them. The magnetic system was working better than the mechanical switch method, but both were plagued with problems; not the least of which were broken boxes with their fully charged six-hundred-volt DC brass lids failing to de-energize and left live on the street surface. We should note, however, that today the system is making a comeback—advancements in batteries, induction charging and electronic controls having finally achieved the goal for those wishing to invest the additional expense.

On Friday, May 31, 1907, at 4:00 p.m., the first electric trolley is said to have "shot out of the barn" on Riberia Street in response to "pressure in the electrical system." It swept down Cedar Street and turned onto Central (today's M.L. King Avenue) and glided straight, true and nearly imperceptively to King. Onboard the "secret" run were members of the local media from both Jacksonville and St. Augustine as well as local dignitaries. In fact, the passenger list read like a "who's who" of regional heavyweights. Mr. Barnett from Jacksonville, the largest stockholder on the road, had mentioned that he wanted to ride over the line before returning home, so the impromptu press run was for his benefit. Mayor Boyce and two of the aldermen were on that first streetcar as well. The secret had leaked out, and the streets were fairly crowded with groups of people who had come to watch the big event. Some ladies waved the car down and were allowed onboard. The car played back and forth between the barn at the end of Cedar on Riberia and the corner of Central and King, as there was no power on that stretch.

The surface contact system had failed them, and though the boxes were doubly sealed with pitch, they could not keep out water. To compound the failure, the boxes were found to be sweating so much even when "dry" that they were prone to being wet inside and fully charged, creating a veritable deathtrap. Even at this early stage, the company was forced into making the cataclysmic decision to bury the surface system and put up the poles and wires for a complete trolley overhead.

A trolley on King Street, as captured by artist Linda Holmes. Linda is spot-on for detail, right down to the offset headlight. She has portrayed several local streetcar scenes, and there are more to come. See http://lindaholmesart.com. *Courtesy of Linda Holmes.*

Workers were rushing to complete the remake of the King Street and Malaga Lines and were setting temporary poles that supported the trolley wire. A rush order was made for proper ornamental poles. More convertible cars, great for all weather extremes, were also expected from the builder as soon as the custom order could be shipped. Four miles of tracks were being placed in the city, and another five miles worth of new materials for Amelia Island was on its way. Finally, on June 15, 1907, the St. Johns Light and Power Company made its first revenue trips on the line extending from the depot on Malaga Street to the foot of the bridge on King. The first full day of operation over just that one short segment added up to 475 paying fares. And perhaps most importantly, Flagler, on seeing the cars glide silently past his great hotel using the nearly imperceptible single overhead wire, was in a mood to truncate his demands.

On September 28, the first scheduled electric car crossed over the drawbridge and out onto Amelia Island. The former narrow-gauge track had been widened to standard gauge with the addition of a third rail. Thus, narrow-gauge cars could continue to serve as components of the work trains as the railhead moved south along the beach. In fact, the first electric car didn't go all the way to the beach but turned back at the lighthouse station because a narrow-gauge train was blocking the track closer to the end of the line.

Work continued right through 1908, as the San Marco and Bay Street Lines were next tied into the system with a piece of track skirting the edge of that troublesome government reservation. When the San Marco Line was opened out to the water works, the company recorded six hundred fares on the line's first day. Work continued to push the tracks farther out in North City, arriving at the Florida School for the Deaf and Blind at the corner of Genopoly Street by the end of the year.

No sooner had the northern extension opened than it was discovered that Central and South Streets were prone to standing water, and the company immediately set about to raise those tracks. While running through a mud puddle in a typical street wouldn't cause a problem to the all-weather cars, the weight of the cars would function to pump the soil under the track as the cars passed. And like patting the sand near the shore, in no time, the water would appear and the track would sink, causing for a very rough ride.

The city and the island were certainly on a roll, and the newspaper accurately augured:

> *The result will undoubtedly be a rapid rise in the value of realty. In fact all sections of the city will rapidly develop in the wake of the trolley car.*

Property in the remote parts of the city is now offered at very low prices and the time for investment is ripe. Beautiful residence sites, which have remained unimproved, will soon command fancy prices and advance beyond the reach of people of modest means. Many prospective owners of homes have waited to satisfy themselves that the streetcar line would materialize. They have the evidence before them now and unless they act soon they will pay a good price for their tardiness. St. Augustine is entering on an era of development, which means an advance in real estate values, and unusual activity in the real estate market should follow.

In 1949, the St. Augustine Historical Society interviewed Mr. H.W. Davis, eighty-eight years of age; he recalled much of the flavor of the city in the early part of the twentieth century: "People got around town on trolley cars." One line ran from the old waterworks on San Marco, across Central Avenue to South Street and then on to Marine Street. There was also a trolley route to Anastasia Island. Davis remembered one hilarious Rotary luncheon aboard a moving streetcar.

In the days before the trolley line operated, there was a little steam railroad, which enabled people to go to the lighthouse. The hotel was built out over the water, meals were served on its porches and below were showers for the bathers.

Late in 1909, the company was operating ten miles of standard-gauge street railway with six cars, the electric utility and a beach resort on a daily basis. It wasn't enough, however, and with such a small population and fares regulated extremely low, the company was sold at foreclosure on October 8, 1911.

In 1912, Mr. Barnett, president of the street railway, went before the St. Johns County Commission to obtain permission to extend the tracks into New Augustine, west of the San Sebastian River to the former city limits. It was conceded that the extension had the commissioners' blessings, and in no time, the track was pushed from the corner of King Street and Malaga west across the bridge and beyond, stopping near the corner of King and Elkton Streets. The *Electric Railway Journal* reported that the New Augustine branch of the St. Johns Electric Railway was in operation by the end of the year.

In 1913, the Assembly Grounds, a beach resort, moved to a different location, and naturally, the railroad was in on the move, providing passenger service for the workers building the new bath houses, hotel and pavilions and also moving the materials. So throughout the winter of 1912–13, engineers were kept busy mapping out the new route and stacking supplies. By January, the railroad was promising that within the space of about thirty more days, it would have the line passable for construction material to flow in. Once the word was given, the contractor for the hotel and other amenities had a crew at work stacking material to be shipped over to the new site. After the line to the new Assembly Grounds opened, things started clicking along in a predictable pattern, but unbeknownst to the citizenry, with just a few hundred fares daily, the streetcar line was heading for trouble.

By the end of 1913, the honeymoon was over, and typically for that era, charges and accusations started flying. Mayor Corbett charged that the street railway was not paying its full share of the gross receipts of the company to the city. He steadfastly claimed that the payments had not been made in accordance with the terms of the franchise. When he didn't get a satisfactory response, the mayor ordered the carline shut down with the object in view of bringing about a settlement. Meanwhile, the traction company officials stated that they had been ready to make a "right settlement" with the city, but that the city officials had never appointed an auditor to go over the company's books to arrive at a settlement. Ultimately, the State of Florida intervened, and the cars started rolling again on November 8 on the strength of an order enjoining the mayor from interfering with the traffic of the railway.

Today, we understand just how unreasonable these demands were on the many companies willing to take a risk in a capital-intensive industry for the benefit of the public. Sadly, this was the course of things in city after city and state after state, demanding more money whilst taxing ourselves and the streetcar lines to build highways. This worst-case national myopia ended up costing us some forty-five thousand miles of clean, electric transit.

A catastrophe struck the city and its streetcar system on April 2, 1914. St. Augustine police officer S.A. McCormick was the first to see flames leaping from the upstairs windows of the wooden Florida House Hotel on Treasury Street. The fire department, under chief Charles Townsend, responded but was quickly overwhelmed by the growing inferno that was being fanned by a steady sea breeze. A call for help went out to neighboring cities, and Jacksonville responded with the aid of the Florida East Coast Railway, arriving on scene some thirty-seven minutes later (and possibly setting an undoccumented railroad speed record for that era).

With the gallant work of the unsung heroes, who fought with horse-drawn pumpers, ladder and chemical wagons and the able assistance of sister cities and their own heroic batallions, the blaze was finally contained. The fire gutted the city from St. George Street to the bay and from Treasury to Hypolita Streets, taking out a large section of the historic Old Spanish cuidad. In 1920, the city finally retired the horse-drawn apparatus and shifted to a new mechanized department with four professional firefighters.

A new city charter calling for a city-manager style of government was affected in 1913, in an effort to professionalize operation of the city. In 1917, a planner from Chicago was brought in, drawing up what we might call a comprehensive plan today. Widening streets, building a new sea wall, a marina and introducing zoning were just a few of his advanced ideas. Another idea was to get rid of that old wooden South Beach Railroad bridge and replace it with a fitting passage for both terrestrial and nautical modes of transportation.

The Great War ended on November 11, 1918, and by May of the following year, the St. Johns Electric Company was seeking to turn its cars running down Ocean Avenue toward the surf, at the end of Third Street, in Chautauqua Beach (Beach Boulevard in St. Augustine Beach today).

In spite of all of the apparent optimism, the railway was a money-losing operation; fares had never increased until the Great War and even then only by one cent, up from a nickel. From 1910 until 1920, the county actually shrank in population, going from 13,208 to 13,051 persons. The growth of St. Augustine within the reach of the electric railway had been

Before St. Augustine's iconic Bridge of the Lions, the St. Augustine and South Beach Railway operated from a station at the foot of King Street all the way to St. Augustine Beach. Sold and changed to standard gauge and electrified, carrying freight and passengers, it was the longest lived of the ancient city's railways. *From the author's collection.*

explosive; the town had mushroomed from a sleepy village of 4,272 to 6,192 between the years 1900 and 1920, yet still slipped from the state's fifth-largest city to its twelfth.

As pseudo charities, most of the large utility companies were content to continue their mass transit operations without cost to the taxpayers as long as the losses were manageable or could be written off, which would give the accountants some wiggle room. And though the Dixie Highway (actually a small system of highways) wouldn't be complete between the midwest and Miami for another seven years, the company was no doubt feeling local bus competition. The upstart bus operators had a prodigious national industry backing them up—one that was starting to actively mobilize against the electric rail systems.

When the city offered the electric company $20,000 for the toll bridge during the fall of 1921, the utility refused the offer. The city wanted to pay for the bridge and then charge the electric railway a $100 monthly toll for crossing it. There were a good many other concessions in the city's bid for the bridge that the railway did not find palatable.

The railway countered with an offer to sell for $21,000 with contractual stipulations that there would be no tolls charged to the company or its vehicles. The most bitter part of the railway's offer was a provision that the city and county abrogate that part of the railway's franchise that required it to operate a street railway service on the city streets in urban St. Augustine. This was something the city had been expecting but perhaps not this quickly, and it was the one item of demand that it least wanted to see.

In June 1922, the proverbial cat was out of the bag, and the city commission met with W.A. Houston of the electric company, who told the commission that the railway in the city was going to quit. Houston opened the discussion and sealed it with a thinly veiled threat to the effect that if the city didn't approve, the railway would appeal to other and higher authority and quit anyway.

For the commission's part, nobody knew if it could even approve such a thing without first taking it to the electorate, but the railway said it wanted an answer in a week.

Mayor Perry had some previous casual conversation on the matter and asked Houston if the city allowed the electric company to discontinue its city lines, would the citizens get a reduction in their electric rates? Houston responded, "No, and I don't expect you'll see such a reduction as long as we must keep operating the city's transit either."

More or less in desperation, a conversation built up around the idea of continuing to expand the line on Amelia Island down to St. Augustine Beach or southward in exchange for the title to the bridge and permission to quit the city lines. This was something that both the city and the electric company felt could be a possible solution, and though the city certainly didn't like the idea of losing its transit system, it was resigned to accept the best deal it could make for the people.

Perhaps in a spirit of avenging the coming loss of the streetcars, the city slapped at the company in July 1922, revoking the additional penny fare that had been approved during and for the duration of the recent World War.

The bridge issue continued to be an area of concern that seemed to be moving swiftly from the control of the railway and into the hands of the city and state. Henry Rodenbaugh, a vice president of the Florida East Coast Railway, had overseen his share of bridges, and he stepped out of the

St. Johns Electric Company Railway took over and strengthened the old South Beach Railway Bridge when it merged that company into its system. Long before the Bridge of the Lions, St. Augustine boasted a bridge of the electrics. *Courtesy of the Library of Congress.*

shadows to help get the bond issue organized to finance a new bridge. It was apparently also his idea that the bridge be a work of art and a fitting gateway into the city during the seemingly endless Florida real estate boom of the 1920s. Rodenbaugh introduced his handpicked engineer, J.E. Greiner, to get the job done.

The city soon authorized a bond issue to be paid in toll revenue for a new $1 million toll bridge over the Matanzas River. For the project, the city hired John Edwin Greiner, arguably America's most famous bridge engineer. Greiner had spent years with the Baltimore and Ohio Railroad and laid out a typically strong railroad-style bridge of riveted steel plates. The design of graceful cantilevered arches supporting both the roadway and electric railway was complete with four towers seemingly guarding the bascule draw span. Construction on the new bridge started in 1925 and was complete and ready for traffic in 1927; unfortunately, by then the real estate bubble had burst and much of Florida was feeling a "depression" before the Great Depression.

There was a wholesale evacuation from the offices of the St. Johns Electric Railway as J.I. Mange, president of the St. Johns Electric Company, was elected president of the Southern New York Power and Railway Corporation in 1922.

ORDINANCE NO. 236
P.R. PERRY, MAYOR

AN ORDINANCE permitting the St. Johns Electric Company, a corporation, its successors and assigns, to discontinue the electric street railway or trolley line in the City of St. Augustine, Florida; with the exception of the electric car line or trolley line from the seawall on the West Bank of Matanzas River, over the Matanzas River Bridge, on and over the Causeway to Anastasia Island, and along Anastasia Island to a point at or near A Street at St. Augustine Beach, St. Augustine, Florida; and providing that the trolley or electric line commencing at the seawall on the west bank of the Matanzas Highway bridge and causeway and traversing Anastasia Island to the Alligator Farm on Anastasia Island shall be built, operated and constructed along said island to a point at or near A Street at St. Augustine Beach, St. Augustine, Florida; and providing that the City shall replace all street pavements removed or damaged by reason of the tearing up and taking away of all tracks, turn-outs or other equipment upon the public streets of the City of St. Augustine, Florida, the cost of same to be charged to and paid for by the St. Johns Electric Company, a corporation, its successors or assigns; and providing further that said corporation, its successors or assigns, shall reimburse the city of St. Augustine, Florida, for all the cost of street maintenance for a width of nine feet upon each street which the streetcars operated during the period that the company refused to repair same…

Section 3. This ordinance shall take effect thirty days after its passage, approval and publication.

Passed in open session by the City Commission of the City of St. Augustine, Florida, on this 3rd day of November, A.D. 1924.

P.R. PERRY, Mayor

After December 6, 1924, the only sounds on the streets of St. Augustine were those of pedestrians, horses, omnibuses, carriages, early motor buses and the occasional automobile. The streetcars had abdicated their throne in the city west of the sea wall. Ironically, as St. Augustine's transit system went through its meltdown, the city of South Jacksonville was still celebrating its seven-month-old Muni achievement.

The city cars had no sooner stopped running than crews were employed in pulling down the overhead and tearing out some of the tracks, including dismantling the San Sebastian River Bridge. Mr. H.E. Mahr, a longtime resident and former county commissioner, protested the destruction loudly enough to be heard in some distant newspapers. Mahr said, "Taking up the streetcar tracks into New Augustine without consulting the people does not seem the right or the just thing to do." Then he added, "In fact the commissioners at the north or south end of the county didn't know about this until the removal was in progress."

Two large streetcars were rolled out of the shop, fully rebuilt in a first-class manner, and assumed their new assignment shuttling back and forth along the old South Beach Railway. The railways of the most historic coast portion of Florida, indeed America's First Coast, had come full circle. Extended to A Street in St. Augustine Beach with a connecting bus to Crescent Beach, the St. Johns Electric Railway continued crossing the Matanzas River.

David P. "Doc" Davis launched the massive Davis Shores real estate development on Anastasia Island envisioned as a sort of "American Venice" in 1925. Originally from neighboring Green Cove Springs, Davis filled in the extensive salt marsh directly across the river from downtown St. Augustine, laying out roads, parks, marinas and canals. The streetcar was an integral part of the plan and was landscaped to blend in with the opulent Mediterranean look of the new community. The graceful new bridge connected the Davis Shores section to the ancient city, and when the famous Bridge of the Lions opened in 1927, the streetcars were there.

Davis Shores was barely off the blueprints when the wires came down—the boom was over. Davis himself was lost at sea in 1926. Forced by the official agreement and bound by the ordinance, the remaining railway would have to carry passengers at a pre-1906 ticket rate. The dark cloud that had descended over Anastasia Island grew darker when the demand for public transit to the beach died with the streetcars. The truncated little orphan beach railway continued to soldier on until 1930 when it, too, was replaced by the supposed convenience, attractiveness and economy of modern buses. Tourism and ridership to the beaches plummeted. The buses ushered in a period of epic failure all along the beach resort areas, exacerbated by the following Great Depression and deprivation of another World War.

Opposite, top: Too late to ride, two unidentified women pose for a photo aboard the abandoned remains of Florida Power and Light car number 205 in St. Augustine. FPL consolidated the St. Johns Light and Power Company into its purview in 1925. The car body itself is lost or possibly hidden in plain sight, serving as someone's garden shed, chicken coop or Florida room. *Courtesy of the St. Augustine Historical Society.*

Opposite, bottom: The St. Augustine and North Beach Railway's right of way across the salt marsh can still be followed if one knows where to search. This view is in the Fort Mose State Park, and the railway's route is clearly visible at the end of this path. *From the author's collection.*

PART III

FERNANDINA BEACH

16
GOING BYE-BYE!

Amelia Beach Company Railway

The Fernandina and Amelia Beach Railway Company was incorporated as a shortline by officers of the Florida Transit Railroad on March 1, 1883. At that time, the city of Fernandina and Amelia City at Amelia Beach were separate communities both politically and physically. The salt marsh of Egan's Creek formed a natural barrier between the two little towns.

In 1902, the Amelia Beach Company was incorporated in Fernandina, Florida, with a capital stock of $100,000, of which about two-thirds was actually subscribed, to construct and operate an electric railway from Center (Centre) Street to the beach. John G. McGiffin was the company's president and chief executive officer, and E.W. Bailey was the company secretary.

Leasing and using most of the former Fernandina and Amelia Beach Railway Line down Beech Street, the new company erected a carbarn in the southwest corner of today's Central Park, while a powerhouse occupied the northwest corner. It had five cars on the roster and ultimately had three and a half miles of track, plus ownership of the electric utilities and the Amelia Beach Casino and Resort. With the communities of Fernandina and Amelia City having a combined population of just 3,400 full-time residents and being in the northernmost corner of Florida's First Coast, the railway only operated during the summer months when the beach resort was packed with visitors.

Fernandina Municipal Railway

With the streetcar line not turning a profit and the national movement toward municipal ownership of mass transit still making occasional waves in the press, to its credit, the City of Fernandina stepped in and leased 2.25 miles of the railway operation at the end of 1915. When summer rolled around, the city celebrated with its very own municipal railway as it hauled happy carloads of excursionists, picnickers, students, tourists and residents.

The beach resort, apparently not part of the railway deal, closed down in 1916, and the following summer, the Fernandina Muni cars stayed locked in the barn—no doubt Florida's shortest-lived street railway.

Finally, on January 10, 1921, the Seaboard Air Line Railroad, successor to the long-ago Florida Transit Railroad properties, filed a petition to formally abandon the old branchline. The abandonment was duly posted in both national and local media. Not a single protest was heard, and thus uncontested, the abandonment was permitted.

It's hard to imagine a scenario in which carloads of happy residents and tourists wouldn't be crowding aboard a real heritage streetcar in Fernandina Beach today. Amazingly, perhaps the early traction visionaries were just a century ahead of their time. Many cities are using a return to streetcars to bolster density, create pedestrian-scaled amenities, manage transit needs and develop vibrant commercial districts. Many cities are also finding out that rebuilding a historic street railway makes them into world destinations. These uses of street railway as a tool work everywhere, every time, even if it's just for the summer season.

PART IV

PALATKA

17
THE FINISHING TOUCH

Palatka, the Gem City of the St. Johns River—a fitting name for this historic place—was once one of Florida's largest cities. Palatka, like its sister cities along Florida's First Coast, had experienced boom times after the "war of Yankee aggression." Thousands of Federal troops either stationed in the area during the conflict or in the occupation decided this subtropical paradise would make a great place for a home. Unfortunately, on November 7, 1884, many of those who chose Palatka were burned out in a devastating urban fire. By the summer of 1895, the city was on track to rebuild bigger and better than before. In 1886, the city completed its reconstruction and started to boom once more. That same year, the Palatka Heights, south and west of the city, were incorporated with nearly fifty homes.

THE PALATKA AND HEIGHTS STREET RAILWAY

The Palatka Street Railway was an apparent rival to the Palatka and Heights Street Railway. The company filed for a franchise to operate on May 17, 1884, but nothing more was heard from it.

The Palatka and Heights Street Railway also filed for a franchise on May 17, 1884. It was issued a fifty-year franchise to operate over Lemon, Door, Carr, Hatgood, Morris, Kirby, Second, Third, Hotel, River, North, Laurel, Front, Adams, Water, Madison, Fleet, Olive, Jones and Plutarch Streets within

Palatka and Heights Street Railway in a seldom-seen colorized postcard. *Courtesy of the Jacksonville Historical Society.*

the city of Palatka on March 30, 1888. Mr. D.A. Boyd was chairman of the city council at the time, and Cook Carleton was the city clerk. The street railway company was required to make an assurance deposit of $500 to the First National Bank of Palatka and complete its first mile of track by January 1, 1889. The charter was approved on April 5, 1888, according to the *Journal of Proceedings of the Florida Legislature*. The franchise ran for fifty years.

The P&HS Railway's officers were William P. Craig of New York, president; S.J. Kennerly of Palatka, secretary; and W.J. Winegar of Palatka, treasurer.

The company began construction, immediately connecting the railroad depot with the waterfront hotel district by way of Lemon and Emmett Streets (today's St. Johns and Fourth Streets respectively).

Palatka took delivery on two beautifully built new streetcars by the John Stephenson Car Company of New York. Stevenson said of his cars,

> *Our cars weigh less by one-half than those made in Germany. They can be procured for £35 less than Birmingham can quote. The cars we furnish Glasgow can be operated from a stable one-third smaller than their own cars*

require. The nature of American woods has much to do with our success. The selection and preparation of material are no light jobs; the process of preparation requires three to four years. American irons are tougher than the English and we can get the required strength with less weight. We use white oak, white ash, poplar, basswood, hickory, beech, maple and pine—woods all easily procurable by us, while the English are obliged to use teakwood. Because their woods are inferior, they find it necessary to reinforce with iron, at the expense of lightness.

The railway opened for business in January 1889 with about a mile of three-foot, narrow-gauge track. It was said the charter granted it a fare of no more than five cents per mile, but as the state quickly moved to regulate streetcar fares, this was likely changed to five cents per ride.

The St. Johns River was crossed by the railroad in 1888, bringing in even more people and industry and swelling the population to some three thousand persons. It was during this era that Palatka played host to a great many rich and powerful titans of American enterprise. As the head of navigation for deep-sea vessels, the town bloomed into a resort for river excursionists and tourists. Hotels such as the Arlington, Canova, Kean, Saratoga, West End, Winthrop and, of course, the five-hundred-room Putnam House were built during this time.

As winter started late in 1891, the Palatka and Heights Street Railway began to expand along the waterfront, reaching two miles in length. The company's annual meeting in March saw the reelection of W.P. Craig as president and Marcus Loab as the new superintendent. In April 1892, the company studied the idea of converting the system to electric power, and with that in mind, it began extending the route another 1.5 miles into the Heights, creating something of a crescent-shaped beltline.

By 1895, El Perfecto Cigars were being made in Palatka, and along with the hotels, the cigar plant added another one hundred workers to the city. The carline up the grade into the Heights was completed during this same year and quickly became a tourist attraction. This pushed the total mileage to four. The company introduced fifteen-minute headways over the whole system.

The *Street Railway Review* was duly impressed, and in 1898, it featured an article saying:

Picturesque Palatka
The extension of the Palatka and Heights Railway Company's system of Palatka, Florida, to the Heights by a semi-circular track of 3 miles, and

Palatka and Heights Street Railway, seen in a popular postcard view. *Courtesy of the Putnam County Florida Historical Society.*

by an incline of gentle grade to an altitude of 140 feet above the city, has made the line one of the most picturesque in the South. Its fame for scenic beauty has quickly spread among the tourists who seek Florida in the winter, for since the completion of this branch of the line the observation cars are always filled with junketing parties. After traversing the principal streets of Palatka proper, passing the palatial homes of distinguished citizens, the gardens, the orange groves budding into beauty, the cars reach the heights, where, 140 feet below, like a gem in an emerald setting, nestles the Gem City, with its shops, its mills and factories, while east is seen the St. Johns, the king of rivers.

Hardly the words of a typical railroader of the trunk line or streetcar variety, the prose speaks to Palatka's charm then and now.

Rumors were rife in 1899; the *Transit Journal* felt compelled to write, "The Palatka and Heights Street Railway has no work in contemplation." The company actually had a great deal of work in contemplation, and at the February 1902 directors' meeting announced, "The company will build sixteen miles of new track and ten miles of transmission line as well as buy new equipment." Yet by year's end, the United States *Census of Electrical Industries, 1902–: Street Railways and Trolleybus* reported they had settled back

Standing in front of Palatka's storied Putnam House Hotel, in spite of the comments "car 2" should have been a clue to the writer of this early postcard; it was not the only car on the Palatka and Heights Street Railway. *Courtesy of the Jacksonville Public Library.*

to a 3.5-mile street route and .33 miles of private right of way. Suddenly, in the spring of 1903, news came out that Palatka and the Heights had reached a population of six thousand and that the street railway was for sale.

There is no doubt that Palatka's rapid industrialization, combined with Flagler's railroad reaching Miami, Plant's reaching Tampa (then being sold to the Atlantic Coast Line) and the entry of the Seaboard Air Line Railroad, stole Palatka's tourism. As the steamboats slowly faded into history, Palatka would continue to add rail lines, shops, yards and factories. To a street railway accustomed to selling tourism, the new face of Palatka was quite foreign.

The annual meeting of the stockholders in February 1907 must have come as a real surprise to the various industry reporters. There were no takers on the sale, and no great expansion or electrification ever happened. A few years later, the city would kill a solid interurban plan backed by the DuPont family that was refused access to the St. Johns River Bridge. The streets were eventually paved over, and the last traces of the old railway

faded from sight. Left twenty miles off the national interstate highway grid, the federal and state highway departments tossed Palatka a bone with a giant four-lane speedway featuring coordinated signals that split downtown, bypassed Lemon Street and annihilated the historic business core.

Today, the gem of the St. Johns is trying hard to make a comeback. There are new waterfront parks where steamboat wharves and mills once stood. New hotels and a Main Street project are positive signs of progress, but Palatka still lacks that hook—that solitary point of international interest. Perhaps it will be like Kenosha or East Troy, Wisconsin; Fort Smith, Arkansas; or Nelson, British Columbia. Just perhaps Palatka will find its future buried in the roadways of its past.

Opposite, top: Tour groups flocked around Palatka's Railway to "climb to the heights" around sunset. At 140 feet above the city, the lights twinkled, the steamboat docks were visible and nearby ravines offered fantastic views and flora and fauna to delight the eyes. *Courtesy of the Jacksonville Public Library.*

Opposite, bottom: Downtown Palatka remembers; its primary business street, bypassed by the highway department, is reinventing itself around its own amazing past. Once one of Florida's largest ten cities, restoration, redevelopment and rail could be the classic "three Rs" as it reaches into the past to build its future. *From the author's collection.*

PART V
GREEN COVE SPRINGS

18
BIG BUSINESS

GREEN COVE STREET RAILWAY COMPANY

The *Engineering News and American Contract Journal* published an article on September 6, 1884, stating that a new Green Cove Street Railway was being organized. This was followed on August 3, 1891, by incorporation of the Green Cove Street Railway Company, according to the Florida secretary of state.

In the late 1880s and into the 1890s, Green Cove Springs became well known nationally as the "Saratoga of the South." Certainly nicknames such as the "Parlor City" didn't hurt. The city boasts a beautiful sulfur mineral spring boiling up at nearly three cubic feet per second above the bathing pool from a cavern some 98 feet deep. Ancient waters scientifically dated to be 14,397 years old spill over a weir and flow through a spring run some 450 feet to the St. Johns River.

About three-quarters of a mile north of the Green Cove Spring boil is Magnolia Springs, and once upon a time, it was probably the greatest reason for the area's twenty-year tourism superfluity. The great Magnolia Springs Hotel was on the hill just a few hundred feet north of the confluence of Governors Creek and the St. Johns River. It was said to be the equal of anything found in the north. In *Palmetto-Leaves*, Harriet Beecher Stowe writes:

> *In the usual fashion of Southern life, it is surrounded with wide verandas, where the guests pass most of their time—the ladies chatting, and working embroidery; the gentlemen reading newspapers and smoking.*

Magnolia Springs Hotel along the Green Cove Street Railway; note the "baggage car."
Courtesy of the Clay County Archives.

Magnolia Springs Hotel along the Green Cove Street Railway. *Courtesy of the Clay County Archives.*

The amusements are boating and fishing parties of longer or shorter duration, rides and walks along the shore, or croquet on a fine, shady croquet-ground in a live-oak grove back of the house.

…We returned just in time to rest for dinner. The dining-hall is spacious and cheerful; and the company are seated at small tables, forming social groups and parties. The fare was about the same as would be found in a first-class boarding-house at the North. The house is furnished throughout in a very agreeable style; and an invalid could nowhere in Florida have more comforts. It is more than full, and constantly obliged to turn away applicants.

The Green Cove Street Railway record is fraught with mystery—not unlike Fernandina Beach—neither city, county nor state records exist in any detail. It is a commonly held belief that the Green Cove Street Railway was the first in Florida, but we know that the line wasn't built until after the third and largest hotel at Magnolia Springs was opened. The 1884 announcement in the *Engineering News and American Contract Journal* fits such a timeframe perfectly and is likely the true beginning of this fascinating diminutive railway.

The state and federal governments were more adept at record keeping for logging and lumber railways than for street railways. In many states, including Florida, the oversight of the various "railroad commissions" was not even extended to include street railways until the 1900s.

In Green Cove Springs, there is also a common thread that says the Darby and Savage lumber mill operated the street railway in 1870, yet at the state level, there is no record of this company having any railroad equipment. As no more detailed official record exists, verifiable evidence records the following local operations:

1877: Dantzler Lumber operated a two-mile logging railroad to Green Cove Springs.

1891: Tilghman Wilson Company operated a logging tram railroad to a camp at Green Cove Springs and moved to Stokes Landing in 1909.

1892–1899: South-Western Railroad of Florida operated a thirty-three-mile, three-foot narrow-gauge railroad from Melrose to Green Cove Springs. The road operated under various other names from 1882.

Unknown Year: J.F. Darby Company operated a logging railroad at an unknown Florida location.

Four other companies would operate independent railroads in the area, but these were in the post–street railway era in Green Cove Springs. They were:

1912: Dowling-Shands Lumber Company operated a ten-mile logging railroad to Green Cove Springs.

1921: Florida Farms and Industries Railroad.

1924: Robert L. Dowling and Son operated a logging railroad at Green Cove Springs.

1925: J.C. Penny Railroad (purchased the Florida Farms and Industries Railroad).

Certainly any one of these might have operated a short connecting link between Green Cove Springs and Magnolia Springs, but to what purpose when wharves and a standard-gauge rail line existed at and between both places?

Try as I might at state, county and city archives; courthouse records; and early media, I was unable to prove the system could have, at best, predated 1884. It is even more likely that it wasn't until the incorporation of the Green Cove Street Railway in 1891 that tracks actually appeared along the various streets of the city. This of course means neither that Green Cove Springs nor its sister community of Magnolia Springs were the first, but they absolutely boasted a street railway that was among the earliest and most comprehensive small system ever built in Florida.

The system used horse cars universally known as hay burners in the vernacular of the day. Others have disparaged the street railway's equipment, calling the beautiful streetcars "carts." Green Cove's streetcars were in no way mere carts; the Green Cove cars were as deluxe as factory-built horse cars found in any great city. Could it be that people once hitched rides on rail carts around one of the mills, as young people of that era were want to do for entertainment? This would explain the local confusion with regard to what was absolutely a first-class street railway.

The carbarn and stables were located in the lot on the northwestern corner of Houston and Pine Streets in Green Cove Springs. Three-foot gauge tracks were laid from the end of the Magnolia Springs Hotel pier past the hotel to the Magnolia Springs railroad station. A connecting line crossed Governors Creek, where U.S. Highway 17 crosses today, and continued southward along Magnolia Street to Clay Street to St. Johns to Bay Street. Another line ran from the end of the steamboat pier in Green Cove Springs up Clay to Houston and contined westward. The Houston Street Line ran from the railroad to Clay Street, then veered onto Clay to St. Johns Avenue. The Bay Street Line ran up Bay to the railroad tracks where the new depot was eventually built.

Early bird's-eye view maps show the street railway swinging onto the South-Western Railroad along Bay Street. While this track sharing can

According to the writer's doubtful tale, when the mule died, so did the railway in Green Cove Springs. In reality, Green Cove Springs had a truly first class street railway with a bridge over the spring run that arguably would have been one of the prettiest car lines ever built. *Courtesy of the Clay County Archives.*

technically still be done between a freight railroad and a streetcar line, today's Federal Railroad Administration rules make such arrangements unlikely. In the days of steamboats, narrow gauge and horse cars in Florida, rule makers were few and far between. The Green Cove Street Railway no doubt enjoyed the freedom to operate up Bay to what would later become the Atlantic Coast Line Railroad Depot, even though it did not own the track. It is also probable that the little horse cars continued to operate along this line after the several failures of the South-Western Railroad and its ultimate demise, simply taking possession of a short segment of their former hosts' trackage between the riverfront and the railroad after they abandoned it.

It was said that the railway had a mule that was trained and would refuse to pull a car without someone putting a nickel in the farebox. Once the fare was paid, gliding along those narrow tracks beside the majestic river had to be an experience to be savored. Unfortunately for us, the story of its demise apes its birth as it vanished from the pages of history.

One doesn't have to simply imagine the potential and popularity of such a line had it survived until contemporary times; Disney's "Main Street USA" horsecar provides us with a great example. Even a much shortened Green Cove Street Railway, originating in the Spring Park, passing the gazebo and soaring over the spring run, clop-clopping another block or two, perhaps to Gum, or turning down Walnut. If it were authentic in every dimension, it would be one of a kind in North America. Green Cove Springs in a word.

Boasting what was perhaps the tiniest tramway in Florida, at the end of the War of Yankee Aggression, the owner of the Hibernia Plantation converted the great house into a resort hotel. A popular golf course was created, and a small tramway connected the steamboat dock with the hotel. *Courtesy of the Clay County Archives.*

Opposite: Who on earth thought this was a good idea? *Courtesy of the Jacksonville Historical Society.*

NOTES

1. The Diolkos (Δίολκος, from the Greek διά, dia "across" and ὁλκός, holkos "portage machine") was a paved trackway near Corinth in Ancient Greece.
2. "Two Days at Niagara," in *Southern Literary Messenger*. This account is typical; it gives a vivid account of the early omnibus industry. This is doubly interesting when one considers a similar sort of "free for all" reappeared within the same industry as it used industrial might to crush the independent street railway companies.
3. Well into the 1960s, Jacksonville was known as the Gateway City, a nickname largely based on its wealth of railroad lines. While it never had the number of railroads, street railways or freight trains that Atlanta (which proclaims itself the "Chicago of the South" within the railroad industry) had, it was no contest in favor of Jacksonville when it came to the number of passenger trains. Either of Atlanta's large terminals would have fit comfortably within the Jacksonville Union Terminal, while Jacksonville Terminal dwarfed any other station in the South for number of tracks.
4. It became an almost-universal practice among street railways to provide amusement parks, usually located at or near the end of a long route. The purpose was to provide a revenue source on weekends, especially Sundays, when virtually every business was closed. Thus the railways could operate 365 days of the year, though this practice was criticized in the industry press as a waste of money.
5. A headway is the time interval between two vehicles traveling in the same direction on the same route.

NOTES

6. "Tampa's Early Lighting and Transportation," *Sunland Tribune* 17 (November 1991): 27. There have long been claims and counterclaims over which Florida city was first with electric traction and which Florida city ultimately had the largest streetcar network. Tampa, by virtue of having returned to historic-type "heritage streetcars" has long rolled out these claims at various media events and historical publications. A good example of this is found in an article that appeared in the November 1991 *Sunland Tribune*. The article stated that the Tampa and Palmetto Beach Railway built an electric line in 1890 that was sold to Consumers' Railway and that "electric streetcars began running to West Tampa and Pino City, a suburb of West Tampa in August, 1893. The electric streetcars that operated over the line were the first in Florida." Jacksonville operated the first electric cars on February 24, 1893, six months before the start of electric car service in Tampa. The *Sunland Tribune* didn't make the claim of the largest streetcar system stating that the Tampa system reached fifty-three miles. Jacksonville's system, as we shall see, topped out just a little less than seventy miles.

7. Eugene Levy, *James Weldon Johnson, Black Leader Black Voice*, Chicago: University of Chicago Press, 1973.

8. There is no listing for a "North Springfield Street Railway," and it is the author's opinion that the local media was referring to the North Jacksonville Street Railway, Town and Improvement Company.

9. Historical paralysis has morphed into this ridiculous statement currently being repeated by the Jacksonville Transportation Authority, thus the city above all cities in Florida, built on the back of its electric traction system, has a bad case of anencephaly.

10. "Samuel Goldwyn," Wikipedia, en.wikipedia.org/wiki/Samuel_Goldwyn. Szmuel Gelbfisz changed his name to Samuel Goldfish after immigrating to the United States and then changed it again, this time legally, to Goldwyn.

11. Ron Word, "Before There Was Hollywood, There Was Jacksonville," *USA Today*, September 5, 2008.

12. Note the name change from the earlier spelling Phenix Park. The park was named in honor of the city's rise from the ashes like the great Phoenix of legend.

13. News release that ran in various papers.

14. All modern T rails are hot-rolled steel of a specific cross-sectional profile. Typically, the cross section (profile) approximates to an I-beam but is asymmetric about a horizontal axis. The head is profiled to resist

wear and to give a good ride; the foot is profiled to suit the fixing system. Where a rail is laid in a road surface (pavement) or within grassed surfaces, there has to be accommodation for the flange. A slot called the flangeway provides this. The rail is then known as grooved rail, groove rail or girder rail. The flangeway has the railhead on one side and the guard on the other. The guard carries no weight but may act as a checkrail.

15. Florida statutes.

16. Today we are on our second incarnation of the St. Elmo Acosta Bridge and the third incarnation of the Riverside Viaduct.

17. "Updating the Accounts: Global Mortality of the 1918–1920 'Spanish' Influenza Pandemic," *Bulletin of the History of Medicine* 76 (Spring 2002) http://www.ncbi.nlm.nih.gov/pubmed/11875246.

18. The Ingle family's brilliance would shine for generations as John P. Ingle Jr. of Jacksonville would go on to be an executive with Eastern Airlines and the longest lived of the presidents of the Jacksonville Historical Society and author of a book on early aviation in Jacksonville.

19. Bus flexibility was a major selling point and is often repeated today as a reason to avoid rail systems. It is said that buses operate freely on any street, but consideration is seldom given to the cost of the street itself or its upkeep. Pavement lifespan under heavy vehicle use is about one-fifth that of rail. On another point, buses cannot easily operate down landscaped medians, on the side of roads, safely in long subways or inexpensively on simple elevated structures. They cannot be entrained with a single driver operating two to six equal sized units. Pollution is also a factor, and while an electric power plant might pollute as much as a fleet of diesel buses, streetcars can easily operate off green power as evidenced by Calgary's "Ride the Wind" slogan for its wind-powered system. Streetcars and light-rail systems also employ tidal, hydroelectric, nuclear, solar, CNG and battery technologies.

20. Brass hat is an old railroad term for a chief executive or manager.

21. Buses are among several remote connections the author has to the subject of this book. Stone and Webster owned the Jacksonville Traction Company and the Florida Motor Lines. FML was sold to Southeastern Greyhound in 1936. The author was a supervisor for Tamiami Trailways Bus System. The Trailways CEO, Fred G. Currey, purchased Greyhound in 1986, and then Greyhound purchased Trailways in 1987, completing the link back to Stone and Webster.

22. *Florida Times-Union*, May 29, 1959, 17–19.

23. United States Court of Appeals for the Seventh Circuit (1951), paragraph 9. "In 1938, National conceived the idea of purchasing transportation systems in cities where street cars were no longer practicable and supplanting the latter with passenger buses. Its capital was limited and its earlier experience in public financing convinced it that it could not successfully finance the purchase of an increasing number of operating companies in various parts of the United States by such means. Accordingly it devised the plan of procuring funds from manufacturing companies whose products its operating companies were using constantly in their business. National approached General Motors, which manufactures buses and delivers them to the various sections of the United States. It approached Firestone, whose business of manufacturing and supplying tires extends likewise throughout the nation. In the middle west, where a large part of its operating subsidiaries were to be located, it solicited investment of funds from Phillips, which operates throughout that section but not on the east or west coast. Pacific undertook the procurement of funds from General Motors and Firestone and also from Standard Oil of California, which operates on the Pacific coast. Mack Truck Company was also solicited. Eventually each of the suppliers entered into a contract with City Lines defendants of the character we have described whereby City Lines companies agreed that they would buy their exclusive requirements from the contracting supplier and from no one else."

United States Court of Appeals for the Seventh Circuit (1951), paragraph 6. "At the time the indictment was returned, the City Lines defendants had expanded their ownership or control to 46 transportation systems located in 45 cities in 16 states."

The suit was brought by the United States against nine corporations for alleged violation of 1 and 2 of the Sherman Act. 26 Stat. 209, 15 U.S.C. 1, 2, 15 U.S.C.A. 1, 2. The basic charge is that the appellees conspired to acquire control of local transportation companies in numerous cities located in widely different parts of the United States, and to restrain and monopolize interstate commerce in motorbuses, petroleum supplies, tires and tubes sold to those companies, contrary to the Act's prohibitions—[334 U.S. 573, 576]. 4 Injunctive and other relief of an equitable nature was sought.

These, with the states of their incorporation and their principal places of business are as follows:

State of Principal place of Corporation incorporation business National City Lines, Inc.; Delaware Chicago American City Lines, Inc.; Pacific

City Lines, Inc.; Oakland, Calif. Standard Oil Co. of California; San Francisco Federal Engineering Corp. California; Phillips Petroleum Co. of Delaware; Bartlesville, Okla. General Motors Corp.; Detroit, Mich. Firestone Tire & Rubber Co.; Akron, Ohio Mack Manufacturing Corp.; Delaware; and New York.

Forty-four cities in sixteen states are included. The states are as widely scattered as California, Florida, Maryland, Michigan, Nebraska, Texas and Washington. The larger local transportation systems include those of Baltimore, St. Louis, Salt Lake City, Los Angeles and Oakland. The largest concentrations of smaller systems are in Illinois with eleven cities, California with nine (excluding Los Angeles) and Michigan with four. The local operating companies were not named as parties defendant.

The appellee companies fall into two groups. The largest, which may be called the supplier group, includes the last six named above. Except Federal, they are engaged in producing and distributing the commodities purchased by the local operating companies, the sale of which is charged to be monopolized and restrained. Federal is a wholly owned subsidiary of Standard, engaged in managing investments for Standard.

The complaint charges that the supplier appellees furnish capital to the City Lines for acquiring control of the local operating systems, upon the understanding that the City Lines cause all requirements of the local systems in buses, petroleum products, tires and tubes to be purchased from the supplier appellees and no other sellers.

24. The company was indicted in 1947 and was later convicted in the United States District Court for the Northern District of Illinois of conspiring to monopolize the sale of buses and related products to the local transit companies that they controlled.

Over 1938 and 1939, the company made purchases in Alabama, Indiana and Ohio. By 1939, it owned or controlled twenty-nine local transportation companies in twenty-seven different cities in ten states.

By 1947, the company owned or controlled more than one hundred electric streetcar systems in forty-five cities including, but not limited to, Baltimore, St. Louis, Salt Lake City, Los Angeles, Oakland, Philadelphia and Tulsa. The company ultimately dismantled these systems and replaced them with bus systems in what became known as the "Great American streetcar scandal" and formed the inspiration for the film *Who Framed Roger Rabbit*.

American City Lines, which had been organized to acquire local transportation systems in the larger metropolitan areas in various parts of the country in 1943, merged with NCL in 1946. By 1947, the company owned or controlled forty-six systems in forty-five cities in sixteen states.

In 1948, the United States Supreme Court (in *United States v. National City Lines Inc.*) permitted a change in venue to the Federal District Court in Northern Illinois. National City Lines merged with Pacific City Lines the same year.

In 1949, General Motors, Standard Oil of California, Firestone and others were convicted of conspiring to monopolize the sale of buses and related products to local transit companies controlled by NCL and other companies; they were acquitted of conspiring to monopolize the ownership of these companies. The verdicts were upheld on appeal in 1951. The corporations involved were fined $5,000, their executives $1 apiece.

FBI Office Memorandum
November 21, 1946
To: Mr. Ladd
From: L.R. Pendleton
   ...a systematic campaign by National City Lines, acting with its manufacturing stockholders, to systems in various cities...as control is obtained, the local transportation company is directed to buy buses, petroleum products and tires from the manufacturing stockholders of National City Lines in accordance with contracts between the manufacturers and National City Lines.

Internal FBI Memorandum
October 30, 1947
Miami Office
   [Name deleted], *Miami, Florida, alleged that General Motors Corp. influenced decision of members of the City Council of St. Petersburg, Florida, by gifts of Cadillac automobiles to abandon electric railways in favor of buses...*[illegible]*...the outgoing City Council hurriedly passed a resolution changing to bus transportation...the transaction undertaken without regard to financial condition of the city and in spite of the fact streetcars provided adequate facilities and were financially remunerative.*

Internal FBI Memorandum
December 28, 1946
San Francisco Office

These conferences held during 1937 to 1940. [Name deleted] *stated National City Lines, Inc. needed additional capital to buy new properties to convert from streetcar systems to bus systems and Mack Trucks, Inc. was interested in the potential business to be derived from such conversions...The National City Lines, Inc. planned to convert the new properties from streetcar systems to bus systems and therefore the Mack Trucks, Inc. was interested in investing surplus funds in the stock of the National City Lines, Inc., for by doing so the potential business or demand for buses would be increased because of the proposed conversion of the properties from street cars to buses.*

)

BIBLIOGRAPHY

Accounts Association. Proceedings, 1914–1937. Chicago: Wilson Co.

American Association. Proceedings, 1914–1937. Chicago: Wilson Co.

American Street and Interurban Railway Association. Proceedings, 1914–1937. Chicago: Wilson Co.

Barbour, George M. *Florida for Tourists, Invalids, and Settlers*. Gainesville: University of Florida, 1964.

Blakely, Arch Fredric. "Green Cove Springs." in *Parade of Memories: A History of Clay County, Florida*. Clay County, FL: Clay County Bicentennial Steering Committee, 1976.

Bottoms, Glen D., et al. "The Small-Minded Anti-Streetcar Conspiracy." http://www.theamericanconservative.com.

Brill Car Collection. Philadelphia: Historical Society of Pennsylvania.

Brill magazine (1907–1927).

The BRT Standard 2012, Version 1.0, InfraUSA. Institute For Transportation and Development Policy, February 20, 2012.

City of Jacksonville. Charter and Ordinances, Together with the Rules and Important Resolutions.

City of New York v. General Motors Corporation, the United States District Court for the southern district of New York, 1974.

Clark, D.W. "Two Days at Niagara," in *Southern Literary Messenger*. n.d.

"Construction Notes—Fernandina, Florida." *Street Railway Journal* 20, no. 5 (1902): 190.

Daily Florida Citizen (Jacksonville). various, microfilm, Jacksonville Public Library, 1897.

Daily Florida Standard (Jacksonville). various, microfilm, Jacksonville Public Library, 1890–92.

Daily Florida Union (Jacksonville). various, microfilm, Jacksonville Public Library, 1881–83.

Daily Sun & Press (Jacksonville). various, microfilm, Jacksonville Public Library, 1877.

Davis, T. Frederick. "Urban Transportation." in *History of Jacksonville, Florida and Vicinity, 1513 to 1924.* Jacksonville, FL: San Marco Bookstore, 1990.

Dixie (Jacksonville). various, microfilm, Jacksonville Public Library, 1910–14.

Electric Railway Engineering. Jacksonville Historic Preservation Commission. Harding-McGraw.

Electric Railway Journal (1908–1931).

Electric Traction. University of Florida Libraries. Kenfield-Davis Pub. Co., 1912–1932.

Engineering Association. Proceedings, 1914–1937. Chicago: Wilson Co.

FBI. Office Memorandums. November 1946–October 1947.

"Fernandina Municipal Railway." *Street Railway Journal* (January 4, 1919).

Fetters, Thomas T. *Piedmont and Northern: The Great Electric System of the South.* San Marino, CA: Golden West Books, 1974.

Florida Department of State, Division of Historical Resources. Historical Reports, *Florida's History Through Its Places.* City Directory, R.L. Polk & Co's, 1921, 96.

Florida Editors Association. "Jacksonville the Gateway to Florida." In *Book of Florida.* N.p.: James O. Jones Company, 1925.

Florida Journal (Jacksonville). various, microfilm, Jacksonville Public Library, 1884.

Florida Mirror (Jacksonville). various, microfilm, Jacksonville Public Library, 1878–85.

"Florida, Palatka Florida." *Street Railway Review* 6 (1896): 113.

Florida Sun (Jacksonville). various, microfilm, Jacksonville Public Library, 1877.

Florida Times-Union (Jacksonville). "Protest Against Taking Up Tracks Is Made By New Augustine Man." September 30, 1923.

———. "Street Railway May Be Extended At St. Augustine." February 7, 1912.

———. various, microfilm, Jacksonville Public Library, 1895–1937.

Florida Union (Jacksonville). various, microfilm, Jacksonville Public Library, 1870–77.

Gold, Pleasant D. *History of Duval County*. St. Augustine, FL: The Record Company, 1928.

Hensley, Donald. "The Lake Santa Fe Route." Tap Lines, May 2009. http://www.taplines.net/MELROSE/MELROSE.html (accessed August 24, 2014).

Hooper, Kevin S. "Green Cove Springs." in *Clay County*. Charleston, SC: Arcadia, 2004.

Jacksonville American. various, microfilm, Jacksonville Public Library.

Jacksonville Florida Dispatch. various, microfilm, Jacksonville Public Library, 1877–89.

Jacksonville Journal. various, microfilm, Jacksonville Public Library, 1922–37.

Jacksonville Metropolis. various, microfilm, Jacksonville Public Library, 1905–22.

"J.I. Mange Has Been Elected President" *Electric Railway Journal* 63 no. 3 (1922): 103.

LeBaron, Francis J. Maps of Jacksonville, 1885 and 1887.

Levy, Eugene. *James Weldon Johnson, Black Leader Black Voice*. Chicago: University of Chicago Press, 1973.

Metro Jacksonville. digital publication in support of the return of streetcars on Florida's First Coast. metrojacksonville.com.

Moll, William. *Southern Traction; A History of the Jacksonville Traction Company*, booklet. San Antonio, TX: Electric Railroaders' Association, 1968.

Oliver, Willard. *A History of Street Railways In Jacksonville*. University of Florida Collection, n.d.

"Palatka, Florida." *McGraw Electric Railway Manual* (1899): 197.

Parker, Frank. *Florida in the Making*. New York: DeBower, 1925.

"Picturesque Palatka." *Street Railway Review* 6 (1896): 223.

Rail Magazine. published by Bauer Consumer Media.

"Railroads and Canals." *Engineering News and American Contract Journal* (September 6, 1884): 119.

"Railway Investments, Florida." *Street Railway Investments* (1907): 41.

The Red Book of Street Railway Investments. New York: McGraw, 1900–1925.

"Samuel Goldwyn." Wikipedia. en.wikipedia.org/wiki/Samuel_Goldwyn.

"Seeks to Abandon City Services." *Transit Journal* 60 no. 1 (1922): 28.

Southern Reporter 84. West Publishing Company, 1920. St. Augustine and North Beach Railway Company agreement contract. September 24, 1890, 1–3.

"St. Augustine and South Beach Railway." *Street Railway Journal* 5 (1889).

"St. Augustine." *The Red Book of American Street Railway Investment* (1907–1930).

St. Augustine City Council. Ordinance No. 21. St. Augustine: St. Johns County Ordinances, June 30, 1915.

St. Augustine Evening Record. "Box System to Be Installed for Street Car Service."
———. "Contact Surface System For Street Ry. to Be Tested." May 13, 1907.
———. "Electric Cars Are Now in Operation." June 17, 1907.
———. "Electric Cars Run to Island." September 30, 1907.
———. "Electric Line to Assembly Site Now Seems Assured." January 11, 1913.
———. "Electric Street Cars Made Initial Trip." June 1, 1907: 1.
———. "Government Engineers Advised About Right of Way." June 29, 1907.
———. "High Tide Washes Out South Beach Railway." October 17, 1906.
———. "Installing the Contact System." April 23, 1907.
———. "May Discontinue Street Car Lines in St. Augustine." June 1922.
———. "Progress of the Electric Street Railway Plant."
———. "Shifting South Beach Railway Track to Causeway." October 22, 1906.
———. "Street Car Service." June 14, 1907.
———. "Street Cars Now Operated to the North Limits of City."
———. "Street Railway Branches Joined." February 17, 1908.
———. "Will Shift Roadbed of South Beach Railway." October 2, 1906.
———. "Work Resumed on Street Railway." October 10, 1907.
St. Augustine Mayor's Office. An Ordinance Providing for the Construction and Operation of a Street Railway in the City of St. Augustine, Ordinance Book 4, 313. St. Augustine: Committee on Ordinances and Rules, June 25, 1888.
St. Augustine Mayor's Office. Ordinance No. 236. Department of Ordinances and Records, October 20, 1924.
Stone and Webster. Maps.
———. Public Service Journals, various editions, 1907–1923, New York Public Library.
Stowe, Harriet Beecher. *Palmetto-leaves.* Gainesville: University of Florida, 1968.
Street Railway Journal (1885–1925).
Terrass, J.M. "Study and Plan of Relief of the Street Traffic Congestion in the City of Los Angeles, California." PhD diss., University of California–Berkeley, 1922.
Transit Journal 1–58.
Transportation and Traffic Association. Proceedings, 1914–1937. Chicago: Wilson Co.
United States Bureau of the Census. Census of Electrical Industries. Washington, D.C., 1902, 1907, 1912, 1917, 1922, 1927.
United States Congress. Senate. *Ground Transportation Hearings.* April 1974.
United States Congress. Senate. *Industrial Reorganization Act.* S 1167 (1974).
United States Court of Appeals for the Seventh Circuit (1951), para 1, "On April 9, 1947, in violation of Section 2 of the Anti-trust Act, 15 U.S.C.A. § 2."
United States v. National City Lines, 334 U.S. 573 (1948).

"Updating the Accounts: Global Mortality of the 1918–1920 'Spanish' Influenza Pandemic." *Bulletin of the History of Medicine* 76 (Spring 2002) http://www.ncbi.nlm.nih.gov/pubmed/11875246.

Word, Ron. "Before There Was Hollywood, There Was Jacksonville." *USA Today*, September 5, 2008.

In addition, more than four hundred articles in local and regional newspapers, too numerous to cite individually, were used for this project. For specific information, contact the author through The History Press.

INDEX

INDEX

ABOUT THE AUTHOR

R obert Mann is a semiretired transportation consultant who grew up in Jacksonville's historic Ortega neighborhood. He attended Jones College locally and Oklahoma State University and served in the United States Navy. Robert owned his own small trucking business in Los Angeles and then relaunched his local transportation career at Jacksonville International Airport with Piedmont Airlines. He also worked with Continental, United and Dobbs House and then moved to a position as a transportation supervisor for Tamiami Trailways Bus System. He retired from the United States Postal Service. Robert was named to the city council in Cashion, Oklahoma (urban Oklahoma City), planning and attaining over $1 million in grants for street and other improvements. As a private consultant, Robert worked with the inspector general of the railways in the Department (state) of Antioquia, pitching ideas for reconstruction and new operational concepts in the Republic of Colombia. Robert is an award-winning author and historian with several books and many magazine articles to his credit. He enjoys sharing his knowledge of city transportation, history and infrastructure with audiences both local and international. He fathered the plans for rebuilding the Jacksonville Traction Company streetcar system, which he first took to the city in 1980 and is still advocating for today. Robert currently resides with his wife in the World Golf Village in St. Johns County, where he enjoys writing, research, canoeing and bicycling.